Praise for *Rumi: Tales of the Spirit*

"Kamla has written an amazing book [in which] she shares Rumi's untold stories combined with her own rich perspective-expanding commentaries, making them highly relevant to all of us, opening doors and windows in our minds through which we can glimpse a different, lighter, more joyous way of being and living. Insights and strategies are driven home through concrete, unforgettable tales that will stay with you as guiding principles to live by."

—Daniel Burrus, author of the *New York Times* best seller *Flash Foresight*

"This marvelous work of a thirteenth-century religious visionary is a cosmic road map that teaches us, among many things, how to cleverly embrace suffering and thereby harness our inner demons, the better to find our better angels. Here we learn that from them both come self-knowledge, joy, gratitude, fearlessness, and ultimately survival and triumph. Kamla Kapur helpfully holds our hand on the journey. The miraculous insight is—it works."

—Thomas Hoover, author of *The Zen Experience*

"Rumi's never-before-told stories coupled with Kamla Kapur's deep wisdom about the journey from suffering to peace provide us with an elegant road map."

—Ken Druck, PhD, author of *The Real Rules of Life* and *Courageous Aging*

"Kapur's style of writing is elegant, her analysis of characters and symbols in the stories is insightful, and she shows a personal intimacy with the parables and the poetry. The result is, as the title of the book says, Rumi's stories to live by— to live by the Spirit."

—Rasoul Shams, author of *Rumi: The Art of Loving* and founding director of the Rumi Poetry Club

Also by Kamla K. Kapur

Into the Great Heart

Shared Sacred Landscapes

The Singing Guru

Rumi's Tales from the Silk Road

Ganesha Goes to Lunch

As a Fountain in a Garden

Radha Sings

RUMI

TALES OF THE SPIRIT

A Journey to Healing the Heart

RUMI

TALES OF THE SPIRIT

A Journey to Healing the Heart

BY KAMLA K. KAPUR

MANDALA
PUBLISHING

San Rafael, California

To the guides

from all traditions

who teach us

how to walk

The Way

CONTENTS

PREFACE

I have learned and grown most from the worst of my experiences. The definition of this learning and growth is the subject of this preface, Rumi's stories, and the commentaries that follow.

The thesis—or, rather, the hope—of this book is that we *can* and *must* turn from being closed to being open, from contraction to expansion, from isolation to connection, taking the first steps toward wisdom, happiness, and joy.

Rumi is known as a poet throughout the world. Few people know that Rumi is also a master storyteller—that, in fact, storytelling is just a part of his multidimensional self. He is a Total Being: man, lover, saint, philosopher, poet, metaphysician, jurist, theologian, guide, psychologist, and phenomenologist.

Controversial fragments of biography veil Rumi's beginnings, but most biographers and historians agree upon a few facts. Rumi (1207–1273) was born in Persia and lived most of his life in what we now call Turkey. Born into a noble family, he pursued scholarship and jurisprudence. In his late thirties he met Shams, a ragged, wandering mystic in his sixties, and the meeting was transformational for Rumi. The intensity of his relationship with Shams catapulted Rumi into a vision of the universe as experienced through the eyes of love. It plunged Rumi into the wellspring of creativity; poetry and music began to pour out of him. Shams had kindled in him a love of the divine that was henceforth to be Rumi's guiding light.

When Shams passed out of Rumi's life a few years later— some say jealous disciples murdered him, or perhaps Rumi's youngest son—Rumi was distraught. After a disciple of Rumi suggested he write down his thoughts, Rumi, it is said, dictated the entire *Mathnawi* over the course of some years.

Situated at the interface between the East and the West, Rumi was poised to go in both directions. His growing global popularity more than 800 years later is evidence of his abiding relevance.

We are all made of one fabric, and what happens to one person happens, in a way, to all of us. Stories are experiences that help us understand this journey called life, and can teach us how to live better, with greater equanimity, if not joy. Though in one sense I am not relating my own stories in this book, the stories of Rumi's that I'll retell are rich with instruction for the hungry soul, both yours and mine.

One thing that all the stories have in common is that their characters suffer in some way. This reflects the cultivation of a perspective on suffering (and perspective is, after all, is what we need to face and overcome the many adverse circumstances we meet in life) that is the purpose of Rumi's stories in this book. The stories also show us that to triumph, we have to observe our thoughts very carefully. Our thinking drives our feelings and actions, and our mind can either destroy or save us.

Rumi does not merely tell us to keep our hearts and minds in the right place, but shows us, in the fate of the characters, the tragic consequences of not doing so.

Suffering in all its forms is integral to the human condition. None of us can avoid it, not even those we call pirs, sages, gurus, prophets, or guides. But the wise ones know that something as pivotal as suffering must have a spiritual purpose. Through the centuries our guides have discovered, through intense self-observation, highly effective ways of thinking which function as spiritual tools to assuage mental and physical pain by using it to their advantage.

As with evolution, we flourish in a favorable environment, and either adapt or perish in a hostile one. Though in parts of the world this environment still consists of one's physical habitat and life circumstances, many people live in stable enough conditions that their evolution takes the form of psychic survival and triumph.

If, in the footsteps of the guides, we concede that human purpose is ultimately the cultivation of consciousness, humankind's greatest gift and responsibility, we will be able to see that this purpose is intimately tied to spiritual evolution.

Suffering's role here is an extensive one. In the labyrinths, dead ends, and happenstances of human physical and spiritual evolution, suffering can expand our consciousness or contract it. Expansion ensures survival at its best; contraction, if it doesn't kill us, can make us ill and miserable.

It simply cannot be that our species—which has made huge strides in knowledge and technology, medicine and science—is a random excrescence, a biological by-product of a haphazard event. We are the blossoming of creation. We cannot allow ourselves to flounder and blunder through life. After all, it is our birthright to live with purpose and meaning. Whether we know and follow it or not, the spiritual quest is, for all people, a yearning. That much of our suffering comes from our feelings and thoughts about the aimlessness of existence is evidence that all but the most wounded of us search for spiritual meaning. Its absence is what causes much of the dysfunction in individuals, families, groups, tribes, and nations. If we give ourselves the choice of prevailing in the face of our physical and mental environments and take on the rewarding burdens of self-observation, suffering becomes grist and fuel for spiritual growth. Our guides have seen through the terrible mask of pain in all its forms, and realized how rich its rewards are. Suffering is an impetus for a series of unfolding transformations that fuel our journey to healing and wholeness, which cultures around the world refer to as some variation of The Way, or The Path.

This image of the path that leads from suffering to peace is central to all religions because it is central to the human psyche's struggle to find a way to serenity, happiness, joy. In fact, another definition of all religions can be "paths," since they give their adherents a passage from darkness to light. All these paths, if we are careful not to become bigots deriding other paths, lead us to that home within ourselves that is far sturdier, more comfortable and peace-filled than anything made of wood, brick, and mortar: the home that is the thrust of all our seeking.

I was brought up as a Sikh. The Sikh holy book, the Guru Granth Sahib, is a compilation of hymns of Sikh gurus as well as Hindu and Sufi saints. The fabric of Sikh history is woven through with Muslim characters. The Sikh gurus believe that all religions are to be revered because they reveal aspects of the same universal truths. The One can be found in the Hindu Vedas as well as the Koran, said Guru Gobind Singh, the tenth Sikh guru. This perspective of the common roots of all spiritual traditions is particularly relevant to our times, when there is so much fragmentation between different religious ideologies.

Why are almost all religions, distant from each other in time and space, so similar in essence as to use the same symbol, The Way? Despite its many manifestations, there is really only One Way. It is the path of spiritual growth that we all have the ability to travel. It is a direction, in the sense of instruction as well as the course on which a person needs to move to arrive at a particular destination. It is the direction leading us when all other direction is lost; it is what we want so desperately to find in times of chaos and confusion—something, someone to turn to. The comfort of having this recourse, this "turning to," is healing enough.

We generally think of thought and action as two different things, but thought is action. It often takes just a tiny, invisible inner gesture, a fraction of a one-degree assent to a particular manner of thinking or remembrance that is the action required to change our view completely. Often all it takes to simplify and solve a problem or situation is to think about it in a different way. The Way is a method of thinking about distress that opens up doors and windows in our brain with a vision of the free blue sky beyond the dungeons we inhabit, and must inhabit, because it is our destiny to suffer. Suffering is sort of woven into our very flesh, perhaps because it serves such an integral function in our multidirectional evolution. The Way is a way to transform our experiences and realities. When we commit to it, then it is The Way that carries us to our destinations.

The Way is treaded by our guides. No path is easy, but then neither is the task of navigating our way through the turbulent waters of life. Suffering, disease, anxiety, mental instability, loss, fears, and death are democratic in the extreme and affect all. Some perish from these perils, and many who survive find themselves embittered by their experiences, living a life of "quiet desperation."

Rumi's stories show us in unmistakable and clear signposts the obstacles to The Way and how to overcome them.

In many instances I have combined several of Rumi's stories into one, added names and endings when they were diffuse in the originals, and recreated them for our times. The categories I have put them in are mine rather than Rumi's, though the organizing themes I've used are ubiquitous in his writings. The narratives primarily demonstrate the themes under which they appear, but on the whole Rumi's tales are far too complex structurally and metaphysically to be entirely contained within category bounds. Rumi and his stories are like the delta of a river that splits into many distributaries emptying into the same ocean. The main argument is invariably complemented by many related ideas. A reader new to Rumi would do well not to look with too much focus for a theme, and to understand at the outset a point that Rumi himself examines throughout the *Mathnawi*, the source of these stories. The story—with all its attendant devices of analogy, allegory, parable, characters, plots, metaphors, symbols, and even words themselves—is itself a device to clothe, express, and delineate the inexpressible Invisible. In learning to see through the story to its message and meaning, a reader can develop a perception of The Way: to see behind and beyond the senses to the Reality of which they are reflections. "How long," Rumi cries to the reader and himself, "will you play at loving the shape of the jug? Leave the shape of the jug, go, go seek the water."

By being thus isolated from Rumi's volumes, these stories both gain and lose. Like a gem worked on by a lapidary and displayed in the bazaars of the world, Rumi is made accessible and available to a modern audience and his enduring worth and beauty are brought before us. But because these tales have been mined from their matrix, so intimately reflective of Rumi's message of that Whole from which, like the reed from the reed bed, we are separated, I can only hope they will lead the serious reader back to the rich and priceless complexity of Rumi's originals.

We would do well to examine our lives in the light of these stories, and thereby discover ways to become conscious of inner demons that breed misery in our minds and bodies. These demons cannot be destroyed. But with the requisite training they can be harnessed, and, in Rumi's words, made to "hew stone for thy palace."

Now listen to the outward form of a tale,
but take heed
to separate the grain from the chaff.

MATHNAWI, Book I, 202

PART 1

EMBRACE
SUFFERING

The Friend is like gold,
tribulation is like the fire:
the pure gold is glad
in the heart of fire.

MATHNAWI, Book II, 1461

When the blossom is shed,
the fruit comes to a head;
when the body is shattered,
the spirit lifts up its head.

MATHNAWI, Book I, 2929

CHAPTER 1

WE NEVER KNOW WHY

Ahmed was sleeping peacefully in an orchard when he was suddenly, and rudely, awakened to find a stranger beating him violently.

"What . . . ? Why are you . . . ?" Ahmed asked, but more blows answered his queries. The stranger did not reply though his eyes bulged with rage.

Stunned, barely awake, and wondering if he was having a nightmare, Ahmed tried to ward off the blows with his hands, but the onslaught was relentless.

"O God," Ahmed cried inwardly. "What sin have I committed? I am a good man, and I haven't harmed anyone. Why then are you punishing me?"

Ahmed managed to run away from the crazy stranger as fast as he could, and rested, panting and frothing, under an apple tree. But the tall stranger grabbed him and began to beat him again for no reason at all.

"Who are you and what have I done to you . . ." Ahmed began, but the stranger was obviously deranged. At the point of his sword he forced Ahmed to eat the rotten apples that had fallen on the ground.

"But why . . . ?"

"Eat! Eat! Faster! More!" cried the stranger, stuffing the apples into Ahmed's mouth.

Ahmed had many questions to ask the stranger, but his mouth was full of apples. Nonplussed and almost driven insane with his situation, Ahmed replayed in his mind all the other tragedies that had befallen him in his life. He came to the conclusion that life was inherently absurd and full of meaningless suffering.

"I curse you!" Ahmed screamed inwardly at the stranger. His stomach was so full that he couldn't breathe. And just when he thought he was going to pass out, the stranger took out a whip and began to beat him with it.

"Run," screamed the stranger. "Run! Faster! Faster!" Gorged with the apples, exhausted, sleepy, his feet and face covered with bleeding sores and wounds, Ahmed ran with the stranger in hot pursuit. All night the stranger chased and tortured him. At dawn they came to a stream, and his pursuer made Ahmed go down on his knees and drink the water like an animal.

"Drink!" he yelled. "More, drink more!"

Ahmed drank till he could drink no more, then sat up on the bank, and threw up everything he had eaten and drunk.

"This is the end," he thought to himself. "We suffer like this all our lives and then we die."

He looked up at the tall stranger and said, "I will die easily if you just tell me why."

Without any words, the stranger pointed his sword at Ahmed's vomit. There, amidst the rotten apples lay a long black snake, writhing and hissing, his tongue darting in and out of his mouth.

"I was riding by when I saw the snake slither into your open, snoring mouth," the stranger explained.

"But . . . but why didn't you just tell me the reason? I would have obeyed you meekly, done everything you asked me to, and borne your blows knowing that my suffering had a purpose!"

"Because," replied the stranger, sheathing his sword and putting away his mace and whip, "had I told you there was a black snake in you, you would have died of fright. This was the lesser suffering."

Ahmed fell at the feet of the stranger, and said, "O blessed is the hour you saw me. Blessed is the suffering you inflicted to awaken me."

————— ✾ —————

Ahmed's experience sounds very much like our own when we suffer intensely, in the way that it may seem unreasonable or causeless. We often "awake" from our seemingly peaceful life by some "bolt from the blue," an illness or death that disrupts everything and causes us immense grief. We feel whipped and lashed by the unremitting circumstances of life, by crazy strangers, friends and relatives we loved and trusted, by loss and ill health. Bewildered, we try to figure out why it is happening. Like Ahmed we wonder: "What have I done to deserve this? Is there no God in the universe who looks after me?"

Ahmed's suffering is multiplied by his inability to answer this "why." He was sleeping peacefully when his ordeal began. But though his sleep seemed peaceful, it was the peace of an ignorant man who thought he had nothing to fear. His greatest certainty, it would appear, was that he lived in a rational world where everything happens for an obvious reason. He hasn't yet learned that life is far more mysterious than he knows, that there are reasons and designs that transcend our knowing. In fact, Ahmed knows very little and cannot see this "terrible" event from the perspective of the Mystery that the English-speaking world has fossilized as "God." Like us, Ahmed is so shortsighted he cannot see what, in the long run, is in his best interest: that his suffering is his cure.

A story about Socrates comes to mind, a story that I try to bear in mind in my own life. It woke me up—stories can do that; they have survived through the centuries because of their invaluable ability to teach us life lessons. You can enter stories, and by identifying with the central characters, live through the events, experience what they experience or at least relate to their experiences, and learn profound lessons, albeit prone to frequent, if not constant, forgetting.

Here is Socrates' story in brief.

The priestess at the temple of Delphi tells Socrates that he is the wisest man in Athens. This perplexes Socrates. The priestess always speaks the truth, and Socrates knows that this statement is false. Socrates simply does not believe that he is the wisest man in Athens. Usually calm and peaceful, even in the face of death, he is so rattled by this statement that he meets with all the men in Athens who he thinks are wiser than he is. He comes away from the meetings with the conviction that the priestess did, indeed, speak the truth; that he is, after all, the wisest man in Athens. Why? Because these wise men thought they had figured out everything and had an answer to every question. Socrates is wise because he knows he knows nothing.

Ah, to *live* with this knowledge from moment to moment! How we forget and inflate ourselves with the "knowledge" we think is absolute! We often think we have life all figured out and dismiss as false everything that falls outside our constricted configurations. Our ego makes us believe we know what the future will be, what the past was all about, what the present means. We feel so superior and smug in our knowing that we know everything there is to know, and all our knowledge tells us there is no purpose or meaning to our suffering; that we are to the gods as "flies to wanton boys. They kill us for their sport," as Shakespeare says.

Life punishes us for forgetting when we should remember—for sleeping when we should be awake. As we sleep, a metaphor for living without awareness, black snakes of negative, hurtful thoughts and feelings slither into our bodies and our brains, multiply as a result of our lack of attention, and wreak havoc with our peace. Looking at it another way, we all house black snakes in our bodies and minds that only suffering can bring to consciousness and expel.

How miserable we make ourselves by thinking that our point of view, our perspective is *the* truth, the only reality, the only story that there is. How much time and energy we expend in justifying ourselves to ourselves, thinking we alone are right. We never stop to say to ourselves: *I don't know. I know nothing. Maybe I am blind to the reason why I am suffering? Maybe there is a meaning to life, after all? Maybe I am not as bad or as good as I think I am? Maybe the truth transcends my knowing?*

If Ahmed had thought this, his suffering would have been life-transforming instead of life-denying. But then, would there even be a story about his experience? Probably not, because suffering constitutes a large part of our experience of life and is the subject of most stories.

So many of our anxieties spring from our blind certainties that the scenarios our brain mushrooms are *real,* and *true,* when they are just illusions, delusions, imaginary tricks Maya plays with her magic, transporting us to places that the demons of our fears and desires have conjured. Like Ahmed, we think, "This is it. I am dying. Life is meaningless." Our perspective breaks down and we plummet into despair. It is precisely the breakdown of our perspective that causes despair. A remembrance of "*I don't know,*" or "*Perhaps something good will come of it,*" acts like magic and we begin our journey upward, out of darkness.

The practice of admitting and acknowledging *not knowing* diminishes our anxieties. The brain thinks it knows something, congeals around that knowing, and won't even entertain the possibility that things might be—or might happen—some other way. How can we possibly predict all the possibilities and the many directions our life may take from the point at which we are? Life is inherently unpredictable. Sometimes a cancer patient is given a few months to live but stays alive for many years. Other times, a young person is suddenly killed in a car crash on their way to their wedding or a job interview. The scientific Principle of Uncertainty, which poses a fundamental limit to the precision of our knowledge of particles, applies to our lives as well. Its function is to keep us humble in our knowledge that we know nothing about things of which we purport to know much; that the Mystery delights in throwing us curve balls that we will be unable to bat but must expect. Or even if we fail to expect them (and we fail almost all the time), we have to prepare to accept them when they happen. And invariably we can't—at least not at first. Our brains tell us everything is wrong. We complain, whine, get depressed, but we must maintain our vigilance to move in the direction of a trustful unknowing and an acceptance of what is. On The Way, these two responses, trust and acceptance, serve us well.

That's why the guides tell us to beware, to watch like hawks the workings of our mind, which constantly stumbles on its knowing and creates a lot of trouble for itself. You cannot harness the mind, stop it, block it, or lobotomize it; it continues to flow like a river through many terrains and levels. When we are unaware of its eddies, it sucks us down into the depths of self-deprecation, self-recriminations, and flagellations; with the force of a flood it multiplies our lack of self-esteem and meaning to the point of drowning. Before we know it, we are tumbling in a vicious vortex of negativity from which we cannot extricate ourselves by our own efforts alone.

We can only hope that the next time we suffer we will remember that suffering brings us a gift: of self-observation, self-reflection, self-examination—of walking, if just a few steps, forward on The Way. Socrates comes to mind again: "The unexamined life," he says, "is not worth living." Pretty harsh words. But that is the standard he has set for himself and anyone who would follow The Way.

Briefly, *the examined life* means that we not only think but also think about our thinking: Could my thoughts be false? Am I right in thinking this way? Can I examine my brain to see if I can think about this some other way that moves past my own self-righteous views to another way of thinking that is more inclusive of the other, more compassionate? So many of our troubles arise because our thinking about issues is flawed.

To accept and acknowledge that we are in trouble is the first step toward getting out of it. The second is to know that we have arrived here by our own lack of vigilance. The third is to decide to do what it takes to get out of it. The fourth is to remember that our suffering has a purpose, though we may not be able to see it, dunked as we are in the murky waters of our circumstances.

But there is a catch here. Our own efforts will get us only so far when we are helpless. We have to solicit the aid of our guides, or the Guide of all Guides, who is no farther away from us than our own skins and hearts. We cannot do this without first remembering that help *is* available. We have to surrender our suffering humbly to the Invisible yet everywhere manifest Being, who all our guides remind us, is the only One, called variously by different religions—God, Christ, Yahweh, Allah, Brahma, Guru—who alone can subdue our pain.

But we *will* forget all our wisdom the next time we suffer. It is our destiny to keep forgetting and keep suffering because we, blind humanity, need constant reminding. Where wisdom is concerned, we are all blind fools, forgetful of our own good: *Homo insapiens*, rather than *Homo sapiens*. Our lessons are not learned once and for all but relearned repeatedly, with more and more faith each time, hopefully, in a Reason beyond our reasoning. If our suffering is because of our lack of vigilance, and our periodic, ordained sleep, it is perhaps because the black snake's entering us is what sends these strangers from the Invisible to help awaken us. Like Ahmed, we curse these strangers, curse God and the Way of the World. Like him, we ask the cosmos, "But why didn't you just tell me why you were beating me up? I would have suffered with more grace."

But if, like the stranger, destiny speaks and tells us all that life has in store for us (you can be certain suffering will be a part of it), we would die of fright. Life shields us from our future for our own protection. It provides us, if we are open to suffering, with the wherewithal to endure, if not suffer with grace.

Stories exist and repeat themselves in constant permutations to shout out the truths over and over and over again. Stories are reminders, little Post-its on the mirror, to-do lists we would do well to reread, remember, and heed. The story brings us back on track when we are lost.

CHAPTER 2

PILGRIMAGE TO PARADISE

In the time of Omar, the second caliph of Islam, there lived in Medina a man called Tasleem. He was a harpist with such a beautiful, versatile voice—ringing out in bass and treble with equal ease—that it made elephants grow wings, nightingales become ashamed of their song, and the dead quicken in their winding sheets and sit up in amazement and joy. He was courted, wined, and dined by high and low. Wherever he went, cheering crowds followed him, bowing and clapping in admiration and adulation.

Time passed. Tasleem's lungs lost their power, his vocal chords their control, his voice its beauty, and his fingers their agility. As he aged, the voice that was once the envy and joy of all became like the braying of an old donkey. He awoke on his seventieth birthday to find that his audience had abandoned him for newer, fresher talent. Because Tasleem—confident in the enduring nature of his popularity—had spent his huge fortune on frivolous things, he was now in debt. His landlord had thrown him out for delinquency, the inspectors were chasing him for unpaid taxes, and he didn't have money to buy even a loaf of bread. And what was worse, he couldn't afford strings for his harp.

Amazed at the turn of events in his life, a desperate Tasleem stumbled out of his home, his unstrung harp in his arms and a bitter monologue in his head. How could Allah, if He was kind, as people said He was, make him suffer like this? People had called Tasleem God's minstrel, and Tasleem knew it to be true. But did He not care for his own minstrel? Did He not blink an eye at the decay of a talent such as Tasleem's? Was there any justice in His world?

As Tasleem walked the streets, no one paid the slightest attention to him. He looked at their faces to see if they recognized him. A few did, but after a brief *salaam* passed him by. They were hurrying to hear their favorite minstrel, a man less accomplished and versatile with the harp and his voice, but younger and more passionate than Tasleem. Despondent and desperate, Tasleem walked aimlessly, uncertain of his direction, his heart crumbling to ruins.

Tasleem's footsteps led him to the graveyard outside Medina. Hungry and weary, he sat down on a tomb. What, he wondered, had his life meant? The world that had bestowed such honors on him was a lie. Even the fame of his youth, so heady at the time, was now only a bitter memory. He would never be able to play his harp and sing, and to not sing was a living hell. And even if he could croak a little, it would only be poison in contrast to his earlier ability. No, all was lost. Suffering and desperation alone remained.

Perhaps, Tasleem thought, the sins of his youth, his pride in his talent and his fame had caught up with him and he was being punished. Looking at the graves around him, Tasleem felt some comfort: At least his sorrow had an end.

"I suppose," Tasleem thought, "I should say a prayer before I die. Death is a big event, and I am a bit afraid of it." Tasleem shut his eyes and didn't know where to begin. He had never really prayed before. He had lived long stretches of time without even thinking of Allah. He hadn't needed to. Weren't fame and fortune what most people prayed for, anyway? They had come to him without his asking or striving. He had felt like a chosen one, special, the favorite of fortune, a child of the universe. But now, suddenly, here he was, a tiny coagulum of matter and mind that had arisen like a bubble from the Ocean of Being, on the verge of dissolution back into it. Oblivion. He would become food for worms in the airless chamber of the earth's darkness.

The minstrel stretched out on the tomb, conscious of the dirt and bones beneath him that were once a man or a woman who had suffered. He had never paid much thought to suffering. It was always something others did. For though some suffering had touched him now and then (how could it not, ubiquitous as air, was it not?), song had always mitigated it: song—his wings, his life, his bread, his drink, his breath, and his joy.

"Allah . . . ," he began, and suddenly a sob arose, dissolving the knot of doubt and anguish in his heart. "You have taken away my song, which was my breath and my bread. How can I live without it? It's true; you have bestowed many favors on this old wretch. You have given me a long life and, even though I no longer have it, success beyond my imagining. You, who have granted me everything without my asking, have taken it all away. Take it, then. It was always yours. Help me embrace this suffering that you have visited upon me. I am naked and helpless at your door. Make me your guest. If I live, I am yours alone, and I will play my harp only for you. But please send me enough money for harp strings—for you in your mercy forgive even those that err and forget you."

Then the minstrel sang a few refrains in a voice racked by tears and, making his harp his pillow, lay down on a grave. The bird of his soul escaped from the prison of his existence and flew away, leaving harp and harpist behind.

Without head or foot, without feather or wing, Tasleem's soul journeyed beyond the pale of time to the unconfined spaces of a garden with mystic, unfading flowers, anemones and roses, jasmines and orchids. Here, without hands it gathered bouquets of undying flowers and without eyes or light it perceived worlds. Without a body it sat by Salsabil, the fountain of the heart, and sang without lips and tongue, throat and lungs, harp and strings, songs of its previous, dreamlike life and all that had befallen it while it was imprisoned in the cage of the body. Having experienced *this*, it could never again be content with *that*—the sensual, material, conflicted world of contraries. His soul was plunged into sweetness, as in a sea of honey, in which it bathed and was purged of its afflictions, made pure like sunrise. Yes, it was happy and content here, far, far beyond the satisfaction of fame, fortune, and even—yes—even of his joy in song. "I" and "me" and "mine" dissolved in a greater unity and identity that his soul—still trying to formulate its experience, still tied to words and description— could only call . . . *Thou*.

Ah, it had arrived home. It never wanted to leave.

No sooner did it have this thought than a voice, the original vibration that created all matter, and of which all other sounds are but echoes, came to its earless ear:

"Don't get attached to this and tarry here. It is just another experience. Depart now!"

"What?" it thought. "Return to *that*? No, no, not yet."

Meanwhile, in *that* world, Omar the caliph, benevolent ruler, man of God, philosopher king, sitting in his hall of judgment, suddenly felt a great drowsiness come upon him. He was amazed at it, but saying to himself, "What a mystery this sudden sleepiness is! It is sent to me from the Unseen, and must have a purpose," he allowed himself to fall into a deep slumber.

In his dream Omar heard the voice of that original vibration, simultaneous, eternal, everywhere at once: "O Omar, take seven hundred dinars from your treasury and give them to my favorite servant, a chosen one, pure and blessed and worthy, who is even now in the graveyard of Medina. Tell him to buy strings for his harp."

Omar awoke, put money in a pouch, and rushed off to the graveyard. He ran from grave to grave, but no one was there except a decrepit old man sleeping on a tomb. Omar exhausted himself looking for a man who looked pure and blessed, but found none but the decrepit old man. How could such a ragged-looking person be the chosen of God? And when all his efforts failed to find another, Omar realized, again, how deluded he was in judging by appearances.

"What a fool I am!" Omar thought. "How unable I am to learn the truth once and for all! But like a child I always forget and relearn, endlessly."

Omar walked over to the sleeping man and sat beside him, reverently and silently waiting for the minstrel, whom he now recognized through his rags, to awaken. And as Omar sat there, something tickled his nose . . .

Gamboling in the waters of Salsabil, Tasleem heard a loud sound.

"A . . . a . . . a . . . ch . . . ch . . ..choo . . . ooo . . . !"

Omar's loud sneeze acted as an urgent summons to the minstrel's soul. It didn't want to leave, but from its pilgrimage to paradise it had learned that even a sneeze had a purpose. So it surrendered to the call, and descended along the gossamer silver strands that tied him to his comatose body lying upon the grave, in the world of form and color, money and debt, taxes and rent, praise and blame. It slipped into its body like a foot into a shoe.

Startled and upset, Tasleem sat up on the tomb and looked at the man sitting next to him. The minstrel sprang to his feet, and fell at the feet of the man.

"Oh, for Allah's sake," he cried, "do not imprison me for my debts! I beg you, sir; kindly let me off this time."

"Do not fear," Omar hastened to reply in a reassuring, gentle voice. "I bring good tidings. Here are seven hundred dinars. Spend them on whatever you need, and, of course, buy harp strings."

This unusual event did not seem too strange to Tasleem, who had experienced far stranger things in his visit to paradise. He extended his hand and accepted the money. Staring at it, he was overcome by remorse and shame. He handed the money back to Omar, then in a distracted state broke his harp against the tomb, and began to tear off his garments.

"Why are you doing this? You are the chosen of God, and very dear to Him. It was He who . . ."

"Stop! Stop!" cried the minstrel. "I am unworthy! I curse this harp that separated me from Him! I curse my voice that led me astray with its beauty! I curse my ambition that cast a veil between Him and me. Oh, I have wasted my life in treble and bass, in musical modes, in rhythms and melodies. While I was busy being famous, the caravan passed me by and the day grew late. I have frittered away my youth in garnering praise! Oh, I have been so full of sin, so stuffed with ego that I paid no attention to Him who is dearer to me than this false and deluding 'I.' "

"Oh, do stop this wailing and whining," Omar said. "It is also created by your ego. *Was, is, will be* are curtains that separate you from Him. Don't you see how you are vacillating between the low bass of despair and the high treble of this weeping? Control yourself! Your repentance only prolongs your sin."

"But the harp has been my problem. I should give it up, retire, and go seek the treasure that is God."

"The harp, fool, is God's gift to you! Why else would he bid me bring you this money for your harp stings? And how does earning a livelihood interfere with your love for Allah? No, your harp and song will strengthen it. God himself sings through your song."

Tasleem looked at Omar. All his experiences in paradise had prepared him to receive this light of understanding from Omar. An exchange happened between their eyes that initiated the minstrel into the Mystery of Mysteries. The minstrel became suddenly still, beyond weeping and laughter, beyond this and that. He was absorbed into the One beyond all duality. The world of form and color became contiguous with the Invisible.

He took the money from Omar, bowed to him, thanked him for awakening his heart, and returned to the bazaars to buy a new harp and strings. He would play and sing for God now instead of an audience that praised and censured, rewarded and punished.

The minstrel went into seclusion and played the melodies that no ear has ever heard. He entered that state of silence and repose where this story, tethered to words, cannot follow.

———— ❀ ————

Tasleem's crisis and suffering is caused by his failure to expect the inevitable course of nature. He is prodigal with money, does not save for his retirement, fails to remember the inevitable and unalterable facts of old age and death. It is his pride in his talent and delusions of perpetual youth that lead him astray.

Faced with old age and the loss of his talent, his reaction is to blame Allah. He does not take responsibility for his pride and the failure of his foresight. After all, we are all given an entire lifetime to prepare and rehearse for the eventualities of our existence with constant reminders in the form of the fate of others in our lives. Our parents, relatives, and friends grow old and feeble, fall sick and die, many of them without the gift of reaching old age. Like us, Tasleem forgets that the Mystery that has bestowed life and talent upon us can take it back at any time. Every moment we breathe we are but a heartbeat away from death. Reminders of sudden, unexpected illness and death surround us.

Things begin to turn only when, almost unconsciously, Tasleem stumbles into the graveyard. The Allah he so derides and blames for his suffering has brought him to the exact place he needs to be to begin his journey on The Way. But though he is sitting on a tomb, on the bones and remains of a human, he learns nothing, fails to self-reflect, and continues to be bitter. The grave serves only as a reminder of the end of his suffering, and this offers some comfort. His desperation makes him want to die.

But he does have a redeeming insight that starts him on the adventure inward and upward, toward wisdom: He stops blaming others, circumstances, nature, or God, and turns toward examining his own psyche. Tasleem's suffering, hunger, and thirst crumble his identity to mulch. The tiny, winged seed of the acknowledgment of his own pride—in his talent, fame, and fortune—takes root there and germinates.

The humbling realization that pride always trips us up is followed by another: that sincere, devoted prayer is always efficacious. His prayer is a sob, a genuine, honest, melted moment in which tears, those blessed drops of water, irrigate his barren, thankless soul.

When Tasleem's eyes begin to open, he sees his own blindness. Often it is the shutting of the physical eyes, and with it the shutting out of shallow, deluding realities, that opens the inward eyes. Sophocles' Oedipus and Shakespeare's Earl of Gloucester in *King Lear* see much further into the past, future, and themselves when they are blinded. We can only see ourselves in the mirror of our souls when our physical eyes, which are turned outward, are closed.

What a massive step on The Way to admit to oneself that one has been a blind fool! To acknowledge helplessness becomes the first movement toward strength.

In the first light of wisdom, Tasleem gives thanks for what he has been so generously given instead of complaining about what has been taken away. Though he doesn't at this point see that even the deprivation he is complaining about has been a gift, we know that it will allow Tasleem to travel further on The Way—that when his time comes, even death will be a gift and an adventure.

Gratitude is the ultimate alchemy. It shifts everything. It transforms vision, changes one's perspective, transmutes lead into gold and gives us the world. Gratitude is the ultimate prayer and praise. Gratitude is consent to our lives the way they are: not a passive acceptance, but a laudation that our lives are exactly as they were meant to be.

Tasleem makes the supreme surrender by giving his life and destiny to Allah. "Take it. It was yours, anyway." Like Kabir, the fifteenth-century mystic, saint, poet, and weaver said, "There's nothing in 'me' that is mine. It is all Yours. If I surrender everything that is Yours to You, what remains of 'me'?"

Simultaneously with surrendering himself, Tasleem asks for help to embrace his suffering. Sleep falls on him like a blessing. It is not like Ahmed's sleep, a sleep of forgetting and ignorance, but a sleep of renewal, of healing, of wakefulness where he is transported to paradise, a garden of undying flowers, and Salsabil, the fountain of the heart. Here he has no sight, the sense on which we rely so heavily to see the "truth" in mirrors that show us we have aged, that we are feeble and poor, that we have no meaning, that our time has passed. The sense of sight deceives us with its false appearances by throwing veils upon what Rumi calls the Invisible, the Unseen.

Tasleem's sleep is the salutary sleep of remembering. It is like Omar's sleep in which he plugs into the Universal, All-Knowing Mind, and communes with the Great Being. There is no phenomenon more fantastical on earth than the insubstantial substance of our dreams. Many of Rumi's characters are transformed by their dreams. Dreams are the mirror in which we see our dreamlike reality; dreams are reminders that we ourselves are, in Shakespeare's words, "such stuff as dreams are made on, and our little life is rounded with a sleep."

Tasleem's sleep is the sleep in which dream comes to his aid, like a guide that carries him to another dimension. He is taken to paradise to experience existence as pure consciousness unencumbered by the body. He becomes spirit, sees his body as the garment that it is, sees through the horrible mask of death, the Reality that is beyond and within the reality we call life.

Our visions of paradise, of a life after death, are just symbols, physical representations of *that which is indescribable.* We don't need to take them literally. These descriptions are what Rumi means by the "chaff" of a story. Take it or leave it, but the grain in it, the hint of a life beyond the senses, beyond the body, entered through the portal of sleep and dream, is True, and promises a harvest.

Here, in paradise, Tasleem is awake because his *insight,* with which he sees the sensory, material world as imprisonment in appearances, false expectations, desires, and wrong perceptions, blooms. But the illusion of the "reality" of this sensory world is so pervasive and powerful that even Omar the Wise succumbs to it. He cannot see beyond Tasleem's appearance. He doubts that a ragged-looking old man could be the chosen one of God. As Einstein says, "Reality is merely an illusion, albeit a very persistent one."

But Omar's timely recognition of his folly saves him. This truthful-appearing phenomenon, eternally morphing, changing, is only an illusory manifestation of the Changeless True.

Here in paradise, Tasleem's being and existence are affirmed above and beyond his fame, his talent for song, his youth. He is steeped in pure being, undifferentiated from everything else, in the essence of Consciousness of which our world is a manifestation. Here he encounters divinity. His own. He has come to the Home from which he does not want ever to return.

But he must. There is more to learn on The Way.

Despite the help he gets from the Unseen, Tasleem has to suffer some more from dualistic thinking The remorse and shame of his past, in which he paid so little attention to the Great Benevolent Being, overwhelms him and he gets entangled in the duality of separation between Him and himself. His remorse that his "I" has separated him from Allah, from God, is as false as his pride. As Omar points out to him, there is never any separation; this seeming separation is a trick played on us by our ego; the harp that Tasleem blames for his lack of devotion is in fact a gift from Allah; God himself sings through Tasleem's song; there is a non-dual perception in which the sensory, material world of money, harp strings, and bazaars is contiguous with the Unseen Source of Spirit, and in which all the disparate, disjointed, thorny elements of our lives are One.

CHAPTER 3

THE GIFT

Mark hadn't seen Joseph, a childhood friend from Canaan, for many, many years. They had played together, grazed sheep together, lain under the stars and shared their dreams together. Mark had loved Joseph deeply, though his mind often got in the way of his devotion. Mark had questioned Joseph's faith in a divine plan for the universe and for humans, and doubted his friend's simple and grand convictions.

"See this coat of many colors?" Joseph had once said to him as they lay in the shade of a tree. "It is thus with our experiences, Mark. The light and dark colors blend into and emerge out of each other, seamlessly. You cannot remove one pattern or color without destroying the whole."

Mark had sought out Joseph whenever he could, for in his company and presence the universe, which he often thought to be a malignant force, became beneficent and kind and the face of his friend made his soul dance.

Then one day suddenly Joseph had disappeared, and his brothers said that a wild animal had killed him as they had gone to graze their father's flock of sheep. Joseph's brothers had brought back his bloodstained coat of many colors as evidence of his death.

Stunned and sorrowful, Mark mourned his friend for a long time. His mourning, however, was colored with many doubts. He had been familiar with Joseph's brothers' jealousy of their younger sibling because he was his father's favorite. Mark felt certain his brothers had done Joseph harm. Embittered, Mark roamed the world aimlessly, traveling from one place to another, but wherever he went, he could not escape the prison of his beliefs. He deeply doubted that a universe that destroyed a person as noble as Joseph, at such a young age, could have any pattern or meaning.

Then one day while he was in Turkey, a traveler from Egypt told Mark that Joseph, son of Jacob, from Canaan, was alive! And not only alive, but governor of all Egypt! Mark's heart somersaulted madly at the news, and as he heard the tale from the traveler, flares of hope, like the light of stars in the black cloth of night, flickered and danced in his soul. Was it possible? Dare he hope to see his friend again? And . . . O joy . . . could Joseph's vision of the universe still be the right one, after all?

As the days passed, Mark became more and more hopeful of meeting with his beloved friend. One day in the bazaars of Turkey he saw a shop full of beautiful things, and recalled a time when as youth they were sitting on boulders by a stream, and Joseph spoke about the necessity of keeping faith in the promise of being God's guest someday, of dining with Him in His bounty.

"If you do not have this faith," Joseph said, "then from His kitchen you will get only dust and ashes. So prepare, prepare, prepare for the Meeting, my friend!" Joseph said, his eyes burning with passion.

"And how should one prepare?" Mark asked, perplexed at Joseph's meaning.

"Sleep and eat little. Stir a little, like the embryo, so you may be given the senses that behold the Light of the Unseen world. And when you emerge from this womb-like earth into the vast expanse which the saints have entered, and go to the court of the Friend, go not empty-handed, but take the gift of this stirring."

Mark had not understood Joseph, who often spoke, it seemed to him, in obscure riddles. But the memory reminded Mark to buy a gift for his friend, whom he now hoped to meet.

He spent a long time searching for the right gift, knowing that whatever he bought for Joseph would be paltry for the governor of Egypt. After much thought and many deliberations, Mark bought a gift with his savings. He turned toward Egypt, his heart soaring on crests of hope and plunging into troughs of despair: Would Joseph even remember him?

But when he finally reached Joseph's door, it was opened straight away, and there, instead of a servant, as Mark had expected, stood Joseph himself, his arms wide open.

Mark walked into them, and sobbed while Joseph held him near his heart.

Later, Mark fed from his friend's table, laden with fruit and cooked foods in abundance. Then they lay upon cushions and reminisced about the old days. Joseph told Mark his story: how his brothers in their jealousy of him had stripped him of his coat and thrown him into a well; how they had later taken him out and sold him for twenty pieces of silver to the Ishmaelites, who sold him to Potiphar, captain of the pharaoh's guard; how Potiphar had made him the head of his household, and how later he was sent to prison because Potiphar's wife had falsely accused Joseph of trying to seduce her; how Joseph's skill in interpreting dreams led to his release, and his appointment to the pharaoh's court as governor of all the lands; how a famine in Canaan had brought his brothers to Egypt for corn; how they had met, how Joseph had given them what they sought and forgiven them.

"Forgiven them?" Mark, who had been seething with rage at Joseph's brothers, leapt up from the cushion and said, "How could you forgive them? They threw you into a well! You could have died in it! How could you forgive those who threw you into the furnace of suffering?"

"Like the moon. When she is waning, she knows she will be full again."

"I don't understand!" Mark burst out. "You could have been buried alive in the bowels of the earth! And it was because of them you ended up in prison!"

"When a seed of corn is buried in the earth, Mark, my friend," said Joseph, putting his arm around his shoulders, "it rises up as an ear of corn. When the corn is crushed in the mill, its value increases and it becomes bread. When the bread is crushed under our teeth, it becomes the mind and spirit. When does anything ever decrease by suffering and dying?"

A mote of understanding glimmered in Mark's mind. He wanted to bow down before Joseph and kiss his feet, but held himself back. His love for his friend left no room in him for doubt. He knew that Joseph, who knew how to make affliction yield fruit, was far, far above his own spiritual state, that the way now for him was to live in the reflection of his friend, and try in whatever way he could to emulate his ways. But how? Did he have it in him, or was he doomed forever to flounder on The Way?

"God," said Joseph, divining Mark's thoughts, "causes all to happen."

There was a long pause. Then Joseph said, "Now, Mark, tell me, what gift have you brought for me?"

"I couldn't think of anything worthy of you! How could I bring a grain of gold to a mine? How could I bring a drop of water to the sea?"

"But come, come, show me what you brought. Let me see it!" Joseph said, playfully reaching into Mark's bag, while the latter shamefully held on to it. After a joyful tussle, Joseph gained control.

"A mirror!" Joseph exclaimed. "And what a beautiful mirror!"

Embarrassed, Mark tried to explain his choice of the gift. "I bought it . . . because you are so beautiful . . . and because you reflect the possibility for mankind . . . and . . ."

"Come, my friend, come. Tell me, why did you really buy this?" Joseph teased.

"Because," said Mark, bursting into tears, "when I see myself in a mirror, I see only defects. And I hope . . . and pray, that I become empty like this mirror, so that whenever you look into it, I will see you in me. With this mirror, keep a little bit of me around you forever!" Mark said, falling at Joseph's feet and kissing them.

"I will do better than that," Joseph said, picking him up and holding him. "I will keep *you* in my heart forever, my Mark!"

———— ✿ ————

Mark suffers intensely from the loss of Joseph. It is a loss he cannot reconcile himself to, a loss that throws a dark shadow on his worldview and faith. Joseph was more than a friend to Mark: He was a guide, an ally in whose presence and with whose words Mark could see a vision in which all our experiences, whether "good" or "bad" are seamlessly woven together, as in Joseph's coat of many colors. Joseph is the friend who reminds him of the Friend who makes all things right. Joseph opens Mark's eyes to this insight, but his vision falters in the darkness of his loss. After

Joseph's "death," Mark wanders aimlessly over the face of the earth, doubting, despairing about a world in which the best of human nature is butchered by greed and jealousy.

And indeed, this fact of reality makes all of us doubt and question the world we live in. It is food for sorrow. Like Mark, we begin to lose our faith when we let the cancer of one loss, one tragedy, spread to everything in our lives. We lose that trust which is essential to our quality of life, at the core of our well-being, health, and perceptions. How ignorant we are to allow doubt to spread because of our lack of vigilance. By circumscribing all events, vigilance keeps them in their place and does not let the poison diffuse through our whole being. To lose this trust is the tragedy of all tragedies, and it befalls all of us at one time or another.

But move beyond this we must. As Joseph says to Mark, "If you do not have this faith (in the promise of being God's guest some day and dining with Him in His bounty), then you will get only dust and ashes from his kitchen."

How many of us eat dust and ashes from lack of faith! The only one we harm is ourselves. We cling to our doubts and sorrows as if they could comfort us when they only vitiate and embitter us.

We need to trust the workings of the universe, to develop what Joseph calls "the senses that behold the Light of the Unseen world," the world that the saints and sages have a free passport to.

To be steadfast in our faith has to be a conscious striving, an unremitting effort to remember the Mystery that has bestowed upon us the bounty of breath. We can remember it, connect with it in tiny ways, for just a few seconds before we go to sleep and upon waking. Islam has institutionalized this act of remembering in five daily sessions of prayer. Doing it just once or twice, not mindlessly, but with total presence, suffices to lessen our suffering.

And, most important of all, we have to accept that doubt *will* return. We have to remember and prepare for it. If we have been steadfast, our faith will return stronger when we realize that without it we become like Mark without Joseph. Joseph lets nothing interfere with his faith: not his brothers' betrayals and cruelty, not his sojourn in a well, not his subsequent imprisonment in a dark dungeon. Joseph can do this because he lives the examined life; because he studies and interprets dreams, harbingers, and reflections of the state of our souls. It is his faith in the basic *alrightness* of existence, his trust in Being that helps him get out of prison and become the pharaoh's governor. All his suffering only becomes fuel for greater faith.

When Mark is shocked to hear from Joseph that he forgave his brothers when they came pleading for corn during the famine, Joseph explains how the suffering they caused him was the greatest of gifts, for it is what transformed him. Joseph has endured and abided through tough times like the moon that knows it will grow full again, like a seed that knows it will be harvested, like the harvest that knows in being eaten it becomes mind and spirit. Joseph has faith in nature and in all its workings, in its messages to doubting humankind that suffering is the alembic above the fire that purifies and distills.

Mark's gift to Joseph is a prayer that he may remain full of emptiness and ready to reflect—like the moon reflects the sun—a sage such as Joseph. And Joseph's gift to Mark and all of us is the high perspective, more precious than all the gems of the universe, from which to view and live our lives. Joseph is the friend who embodies the Friend without whom we roam the world alone and lost.

CHAPTER 4

TAMING THE TIGER

A dervish braved a long and arduous journey through scorching desert and frightening forest, over steep mountains and down dangerous gorges to visit Sheikh Abu Hasan, of whose saintliness he had heard a great deal. The dervish wanted to be his disciple, and to learn from him how he could be a saintly person.

Though his suffering on the quest was considerable, nothing compared to what he faced after knocking on the sheikh's door.

"What do you want?" said the sheikh's wife, opening the door with a rolling pin in her hand and patches of white flour on her scowling face. Loose wisps of white hair escaped from under her black head scarf above eyes blazing with hostility.

"Kind woman . . . ," the dervish began, hoping the rolling pin meant some bread at least.

"Skip the compliments. Ask your business and be on your way," she barked.

"I have traveled long and hard for one small glimpse of the holy saint Sheikh Abu Hasan . . ."

"Holy!" cried the woman, her face contorted into a snarl. "Holy! That scoundrel who deludes everyone into worshipping his holiness! That weak and miserable man a saint?! Don't you have better things to do? You could have spared yourself a lot of trouble. Now be on your way and stop wasting my time!"

"Please!" the dervish said before she could shut the door in his face. "I have come a long way. I wish to meet him."

"Why do you want to meet that impostor and parasite? While I cook and clean and mend, he is busy spouting philosophy and beating his own drum loudly to the world. His words are hollow, his wisdom a sham!"

"The man you call an impostor and parasite is a shining light, woman!"

"You must have hair growing out of your eyeballs, stupid man, to see this shining light. Shining light, indeed, like the bottom of my skillet!"

"His splendor has reached east and west and you don't know it?"

"East and west! Is that how far the sound of his drum has reached? He deserves a knock on his head, like this, that will show him the stars!" Abu Hasan's wife hit the dervish on the head with her rolling pin.

The dervish lunged at her with a primitive, animal energy that surged within him. He felt the urge to tear her to pieces with his bare hands, but, remembering who she was, controlled himself. He couldn't restrain himself from cursing her, however.

"You blithering old hag! You should be grateful to be a dog in his house!"

Hasan's wife screwed up her face and spat at the dervish.

"I spit at you and spit at him!" she hissed.

"If you weren't his wife, I would tear you to pieces, you . . .

devil!" roared the dervish. "May your lips and mouth and throat rot for spitting at the moon and the sky! What a disgrace, a man like him married to a rotten, maggot-infested corpse like you!"

The woman hit him again with the rolling pin, and then slammed the door in his face.

"I'm not a cloud that you can chase away so easily, you beast! Your husband . . . ugh, it makes me want to vomit that he's paired with you! An angel of God, married to the devil! But you won't make me turn back from him," the dervish screamed. "Don't think your ugliness will keep me from seeking him till the end of my days!"

"Seek him in hell!" screamed the wife from inside.

Fuming with rage, the dervish threw himself at the door, which was locked firmly. He turned away, terribly agitated and confused, and upset at his agitation.

He sat outside the door for a while, his head clasped in his hands, his heart in turmoil over his violent inclinations. Had he been wrong about the sheikh? Was his arduous journey wasted? If the sheikh were really as enlightened as they said he was, would he be married to such a harridan? Perhaps the sheikh was married to her only out of lust. The dervish could see how his wife must have been beautiful once. Had he failed in his quest? Should he just go home?

But the dervish was not willing to turn back just yet. He found a kind woman in the village who fed him and told him the sheikh had gone to the hills nearby to collect firewood. The dervish went to the forest, his heart, like straw, aflame with doubt and smoking as it burned.

The dervish, so lost in his thoughts and perplexity, became aware of a loud growling close by. Suddenly, a large, powerful tiger burst out of the underbrush and leaped on him. The dervish tumbled into the thorny bushes in fear, and heard a voice above him say in a gentle, sweet voice:

"Easy, easy. Leave him alone. He has come to meet me."

The dervish opened his eyes and found himself staring into the wide-open red jaws of a fierce tiger carrying wood on his back. Upon the sticks sat a turbaned man with a flowing white beard. In his hand was a long, black whip, which moved and writhed with a life of its own. The dervish looked closer and saw it was a serpent.

The dervish sat up and looked at Abu Hasan in astonishment. A soft, warm, tender light played about his glowing face and beard. Had his search for the saint brought him to a strange, mystic, magical world where the impossible was true, the dervish wondered, or was he just dreaming?

"So, you've met her?" Abu Hasan said with a laugh. "And she has filled you with rage, smoke, and doubt? Don't be overwhelmed by the tigers of your doubt, my friend. Ride them."

"But how can such an injustice . . . such disharmony . . . so much . . . filth . . . ," the dervish sputtered, unable to formulate his bewilderment at this marriage of opposites.

"Burdens are from God, and everything has a purpose," Abu Hasan smiled. "She keeps me humble."

"But she is so very vile . . ."

"Ah, you argued with her. You wanted to make her see the light, to change her! No, you should have kept your mouth shut. There is no winning with her."

"But God should have given you someone sweet and kind! God should not have given you so much suffering!"

"Ah, but if God hadn't mated me with her," Abu Hasan said with a laugh, "how would I have gained the strength to tame this tiger?"

———— ✾ ————

Many men I know love this story. My father, if he were alive to read it, would have loved it, too. My mother, though not as vituperative and foul-mouthed as the sheikh's wife, was undoubtedly a shrew. She resented all the time my father spent writing his articles on Sikhism so much that she forced him out of the house to do it elsewhere. All my queries to her about why she did this went unanswered. I had no doubt that it was a combination of reasons. The first: her resentment that, even though she was very bright and had been offered a scholarship to study further, she was yanked out of school at sixteen by her father, who believed marriage was best for girls. Secondly, she resented my father's preoccupation with spiritual matters because they excluded her. She was spiritual too, but her spirituality did not exclude materiality and the good life, while my father prided himself on being a yogi. It is my belief that spirituality that does not embrace the rich a-rationality and confusion of the female mystery-infused matrix is not worth the paper it is written on.

To shrew-ize women is a tendency even in Rumi's stories. Undoubtedly this story perpetuates the myth of the wife as shrew and is misogynistic. My own experiences with shrews and my own occasional shrewishness have made me see how they are inevitable in a patriarchal system that marginalizes, undermines, and disrespects women, a system that deprives them of the education and freedom to examine their lives and become copartners with men in the business of living. Shrews are women with unrealized potential whose anger against the system turns toxic to themselves and their partners. A shrew is a woman who was never taught The Way.

The sheikh's wife is jealous and resentful that her husband has been given the wherewithal to arrive at the very pinnacle of his power as a spiritual being while all she does is cook, clean, and mend. There is nothing inherently wrong with these activities. On the contrary, they can be joyous when one is not compelled to do them, when they are a matter of *choice* within the framework of freedom.

Having mentioned this so it wouldn't hijack my discourse on suffering, I can proceed with the commentary. But let's not gloss over the fact that the sheikh's wife suffers intensely. What else could account for her behavior toward the poor dervish? She takes out her anger on her husband's admirer and refuses to tell him where he may find the saint whom he has undertaken a long journey to meet.

After the dervish has been tortured by the sheikh's wife mentally and physically, he finds a kind woman in the village who tells him where to find what he is seeking. I wonder if she is kind because love, not a spiritual quest, is her husband's aim. Love, which is the opposite of power, is as spiritual as spirituality gets. I believe there is no higher form of it. Rumi says, "Whether love be earthly or heavenly, it leads us yonder." Love opens us up to take in other people, even strangers. It makes us compassionate, generous, expansive enough to see the divine and embrace it within ourselves in the here and now.

The sheikh suffers too, from having such a partner. She is not giving him any love, that's for sure, but waiting for him to love her first. But he has been unable to do so, and I don't know whether we can fault him for it. It is the chicken-and-egg conundrum that we have no answers for. What comes first, the getting or the giving of love? Who knows why some are able to love easily and others have to wait to be loved first? Some say those who did not get love cannot give it, that those who have been hurt in the past cannot reach out.

But the psychiatrist Robert Jay Lifton, in his book *The Protean Self*, whose thesis is that we need to be more fluid and many-sided to survive, says that in his experience with group therapy, he has come to the conclusion that "while the protean self [which fluidly shifts from one manner of being to another] may have experienced much pain and trauma during and after childhood, it is able to transmute that trauma into various expressions of insight, compassion, and innovation." It is worth our while to be flexible, protean, and open to change through love and trust because it is the precondition of transformation.

But we must leave this question of nature versus nurture, fruitful as it is and cause for so much wondering by philosophers and psychologists, and continue on the path of being open instead of closed, expanded instead of contracted, so we can move on to greater wisdom and happiness.

Whatever the cause, the sheikh, in contrast to his wife, has been given, or has taken, the tools to extract the very juice of suffering inflicted by a vitriolic partner. He knows well the transformational role of suffering. In fact, it is because of his wife that he has become who he is, a world-renowned Master. He has learned not to argue with or try to change her and instead has harnessed the energy generated by his anger to fuel his spiritual quest, to tame the fierceness within and without.

But let us reflect on the fact that his achievement earns him power, strength, and miracle-making rather than love.

PART 2

PRAY

Do not put musk on your body,
rub it on your heart.
What is musk?
The holy name
of the Glorious God.

MATHNAWI, Book II, 267

By my hand
the seemingly impossible
is brought to pass,
and wings are restored
to the bird whose plumes
were torn away.

MATHNAWI, Book II, 1917

CHAPTER 5

THE CUP OF PRAISE

Jalammudin, a musician, depressive and sorrowful by nature, was advised by his priest, who was very knowledgeable about theology and sacred law, to pray regularly. Jalammudin could not see how so much muttering into one's beard could accomplish anything, let alone rid one of depression. But one night, mad and suicidal, he sat up and called out to God. "Allah! Allah! Allah!" he cried all night till his lips grew sweet with praise.

But then Iblis, the devil, said to him: "Stop this noisy babbling, like the braying of an ass! What does it accomplish? Do you hear anyone responding to you when you say, 'Allah! Allah! Allah!'? Does your Allah ever say, 'Here I am'?"

"No," admitted Jalammudin.

"You're praying to someone who doesn't exist, you idiot. Why waste your breath?"

Brokenhearted, Jalammudin ceased to call upon Allah. Now he was really alone, and there was no one he could turn to in his sorrow. Weeping in despair, he lay his head on a stone, and fell asleep.

Jalammudin dreamed he was going somewhere but kept stumbling on a thick, cumbersome iron chain that was entangled around his feet and legs. He came to a crystal-clear pond and wanted to drink from it to assuage a fierce thirst, but he couldn't. He understood why when he looked at his reflection in the pond and saw that a lock, tied to the end of the chain, pierced his lips and tongue.

In the distance the invisible air coagulated into a form, and a man in robes rippling like water floated into the realm of matter from the Invisible. He came toward Jalammudin and stood before him. In his dream Jalammudin recognized him as al-Khadir, the guide to wayfarers and the creative spirit of rivers.

"Why didn't you pray before sleeping?" al-Khadir asked him.

Jalammudin wanted to say to al-Khadir, "Because whenever I say 'Allah,' He never responds with 'Here I am.' " But all he could do was stammer and make mumbling sounds with his shackled voice.

Knowing Jalammudin's heart, al-Khadir replied: "God has said, 'O human, every time you say *Allah*, I say *Here I am*. The two are not separate. Beneath every *O Lord* of yours is my *Here I am.*' "

Jalammudin motioned frantically to al-Khadir.

"Yes, I know you are thirsty. Listen, Jalammudin, I will tell you a story."

In his dream Jalammudin sat up and listened to the tale.

"A depressed, sorrowful, doubt-filled man, thirsty as a fish, sat on top of the high wall of a prison on the banks of a stream. He despaired for his life, of ever having his thirst quenched, for the wall was very high, and the stream was oh so very far away. Many times he thought about hurling himself from the heights and ending his life."

Jalammudin nodded furiously, as if to say, "Yes, yes, I understand."

"Suddenly the thirsty man wrenched a brick with his bare hands from the masonry of the wall and hurled it at the stream," al-Khadir continued. "The sound of the water came to his ears like the voice of a long-forgotten beloved. It intoxicated him, like wine. The sound gave him so much relief and pleasure that he began to tear away the bricks of the wall of his prison and fling them at the stream. The sound of water was sweeter to him than the sound of the rebab, that most wonderful of musical instruments. It was like Israfil's trumpet on the day of resurrection, the sound of rain in a desert, the jangling of keys to a prisoner. With every brick he tore off, he came closer and closer to the water."

Muttering incoherently, Jalammudin got up and began to pull at his lock, but it stubbornly sealed his mouth as the chain entangled his legs.

"O Jalammudin! Prayer is the key!" al-Khadir said, looking deeply into Jalammudin's eyes. "How then shall a thirsty man fail to pray? Tear away the walls that keep you from the water, O despairing, desperate man! Tear them away with the folded hands of prayer!"

In the deep recesses of the shadows of his dreaming mind, Jalammudin whispered silently to himself, "Allah!" Instantly, the lock on his mouth flung open, and the chains melted away to air. Jalammudin knelt and drank deep and long from the cool, clear pond. Having drunk his fill, he awoke from his dream.

The sun was about to rise in a sky filling with the first, soft colors of morning. A cool breeze was blowing in from the mountains. Jalammudin washed his hands and feet with water from a jar, brought out his prayer mat, sat reverently upon it, and quaffed fervently from the cup of praise.

—— ✿ ——

Jalammudin has a tendency, like many of us, to fall into depressions. Helpless to pull himself up by his own bootstraps, he has enough sense to seek help. How many of us thrash about in the sinking sands of despair without seeking aid, without even knowing that we do have recourse, that help *is* available! Jalammudin turns to his priest for advice. This choice is his first baby step toward putting his life back on track. Fortunately for him, the priest deserves his office, and gives Jalammudin excellent advice: Pray.

Jalammudin listens to and obeys the priest. This is a huge step. The role of listening and obeying cannot be overstated on The Way. It is central to every religion. In his root prayer, Sikhism founder Guru Nanak lays great emphasis on listening, paying attention, and obeying, putting precious healing words in the treasure chest of the mind. He says if an acolyte listens to and obeys just one word of the guru, his mind is filled with diamonds, rubies, and pearls—metaphors for our greatest wealth and our foremost survival tool: wisdom. In the Torah, the often repeated word *shema* means to listen, pay attention, obey. Judaism teaches that we cannot see God, but we can hear him. All Hindu scripture is called *shruti*, which means "that which is heard." The Bible states, "Faith comes from hearing." Rumi, speaking in unforgettable images, says, "Receive my words with an open ear and I will make you resplendent earrings of gold studded with gems."

Listening, which always involves paying close and deliberate attention, can improve all aspects of our lives, enabling us to get along better with our significant others, friends, colleagues, and family, all of which contributes to our well-being.

Obeying is central to all religions. The word *Islam* means "submission"; Sikhs use the word *hukam*, meaning "divine command"; Christians and Jews say, "Thy will be done."

The word and concept *obey* has been given a bad rap in our day and age, understandably so when applied to unquestioning subservience to our political, religious, social, and educational institutions. Obedience is a virtue only when it isn't coerced but voluntary, when it is a *conscious* choice. When our mental and physical health, our very life is at stake, when we admit to ourselves that we are floundering on The Way, obedience to a guide becomes imperative.

Jalammudin obeys the priest. He prays till his lips grow "sweet with praise."

Prayer, whatever the reason for it, is a hotline to the Being, Guide of Guides, our own Higher Self, who comes whenever we call, though it doesn't always seem so. Sometimes when we pray our suffering ends, and sometimes, as is the case with Jalammudin, we continue to suffer because we have not arrived at the softness and pliability needed for the sowing of important truths. But if we pledge to suffer consciously, humbly, trusting that our suffering is in fact a healing, we are given the courage to endure. For on The Way, endurance is everything.

To be utterly honest, left to myself, I am unable to endure. I falter, despair, panic. Though I speak about suffering as the guides speak of it, I must admit I do not like to suffer. My not liking it does not keep it away from me, however. If anything, resisting it prolongs my misery. When I am suffering I am helpless to do anything but ache. No wisdom comes to my rescue. Though I often do not know the cause of my suffering, there are some causes I am almost always able to identify: too much of daily practicalities without the balancing effects of something soulful, too many people in my path, too much talk and superficial socializing, too much noise. A lifetime of observing my limits is teaching me to stop, pull back, say no to my many tasks and engagements, to make space and time in which I can perform the most important of functions—turn my gaze inward, turn toward the divine in me, and sing songs, however well or badly, of humble prayer and praise. Any lifestyle that does not afford time for this non-activity may be a lifestyle, but not a life.

Prayer and praise, through music and song especially, connect one to the Being in an immediate way. The Sufis delight in it as being the fastest shortcut on The Way. Singing is at the very heart of Sikhism. "No one and nothing stands between You and me," Kabir sings. Most church services include singing, of which the gospels are the greatest manifestations of passion. No Hindu temple gathering is complete without the singing of *bhajans* (devotions). When we sing we tap into this connectedness, heart to precious heart.

When we pray, whether through song, prose, or inner dialogue, we remove intermediaries and address ourselves directly to the godhead: to You, with the type of intimacy we reserve for the closest of our relationships. In languages with a formal word for *you*, it is often the intimate term we use instead when praying. It is only when we speak about God to others do we objectify the deity as *him*, or *her*, all those gender-non-neutral pronouns. Speaking to his audience, Rumi says, "Lift the veil and speak nakedly, for I do not wear a shirt when I sleep with my Adored One."

When we sing, listen to, or recite prayers with an open heart, with faith and love, we turn to the very source, the giver and fulfiller of our desires, the inflicter and soother of our agitation and anxieties. Rumi knows, as does his character Jalammudin, that prayer moves and stirs, like a vivifying force, the stagnant waters of our souls.

Jalammudin's prayer isn't just "Give me, give me, help, help" (though this is also a very legitimate and most repeated prayer!), but praise. We praise when we are grateful and acknowledge that, despite our adverse circumstances, we have been given a lot, in countless material and physical ways, especially the tremendous, indescribable gift of consciousness, that immaterial something that has birthed this splendid Multiverse and ourselves within it. We have inherited, together with our experience of life, the ability to watch, participate in, and, as active agents, transform our experiences from "bad" and "unbearable" to "good" and "healthy."

Jalammudin has reached as far as praise—and it *is* far. But then Iblis, the devil, who hates the good and the beautiful and puts up many resistances and obstacles on The Way, begins to tempt Jalammudin to the other side. And Jalammudin is foolish enough to listen to him.

Listening, like everything else in this conflicted world woven with light and dark, is a double-edged sword. We can listen to words that make us lose The Way, or ones that put us back on it. The criteria for distinguishing between the two is whether the words suck us on a downward spiral of despair or give us wings. Iblis's words and reasoning do the former to Jalammudin.

The Judeo-Christian-Islamic traditions objectify the devil, placing him as a force outside us, a dark being that lures us into all sorts of trouble. But psychology and the guides tell us he is part of us, tempting and corrupting us from within. Iblis is nowhere if not in our heads and hearts. The Eastern traditions believe that even the darkness of suffering is sent to us by the One Being— One despite its yin and yang, dark and light, death and life.

Listening to Iblis, who is the unchecked negative stream of his thoughts, Jalammudin begins to doubt again.

Doubt is an in-house phenomenon, inevitable and necessary. It is born from our God-given gift of reasoning. If we didn't have it, all the tyrannical forces both within and without that try to control and subjugate us would lead us terribly astray. Without doubt, without a healthy exercise of our reasoning, without wrestling with this demon, we would never achieve the power, strength, confidence, and trust to continue on The Way. Doubt tests us and gives us blessed choice. And each time we choose The Way again, our path becomes easier.

We have to drink the dregs of doubt before we can arrive at the crossroads where we're forced to choose: Either we stay with doubt and paralysis or we take the leap of faith. And it *is* a leap, a mighty, muscular leap from the sunless to the sunny side of experience, from our small egos that isolate and alienate us to something more transcendent of which we are an indissoluble part.

Jalammudin, too, has to drink the bitter dregs of doubt before he can be affirmed in his faith. By surrendering to doubt instead of to the priest who has given him a tool, a magic mantra to deal with his depression and triumph over the darkness that must be encountered on The Way, he prolongs his depression. Jalammudin is unable to make the leap, having forgotten that when he prays his lips and heart taste sweetness, and he falls instead into depression again. Brokenhearted, Jalammudin turns away from his priest's advice, turns away from meaningful, mindful prayer, more depressed *and* alone.

It is surprising that Jalammudin falls asleep. But perhaps his one, sweet experience with prayer has already called the guide to his aid. Help from the Invisible is on its way.

But first Jalammudin has to confront and acknowledge the state of his soul, shown to him in unmistakable images in his dream. Weighted down by a heavy chain around his neck, a lock through his lips, Jalammudin is unable to quench his severe thirst with the crystal water at his feet.

How often I feel the shackles of the lock through my own lips! How often as I navigate my own depressions am I unable to pray! Even the mouth of my heart that so often communes silently, speaking to itself, is sewn shut! Then I am reminded of something the Christian saint Teresa of Avila said: Prayers are like money in the bank; we pray when we can so that when we can't, we have something to draw from. Sooner or later help *is* sent to remind us of what we must do, how we must think, as al-Khadir, guide to lost souls, the spirit of water, is sent to Jalammudin in his dream, materializing out of unseen air, to tell him the story that rescues him.

It is significant that al-Khadir is the spirit of water, elementary to all existence. Not only does water quench our thirst and help us perform all sorts of necessary daily activities in its literal materiality, but it is the greatest of our metaphors, standing for so many aspects of our soul. It is fluid, never static, and stands for the movement and processes of our psychic life. When we are stagnating in one state, water is a reminder that we must do everything to flow again. Prayer is active action. It is both chemistry and alchemy. In giving us a precious place, altar, temple within or outside ourselves to turn to, prayer is the catalyst that makes us flow again.

The guide al-Khadir comes to make our prisoner a free man with the message that two seemingly separate things—our remembering and calling out God's name, and God's response—are in truth one, and simultaneous. That is why God's name is so central in all the Eastern and Western religions. Name is remembrance; name is connection; name is evocation, bringing into presence the absent and forgotten; name is help when we need it most; name, calling out to our Beloved, is prayer; name itself is aid, food, sustenance in the highest.

To remind Jalammudin to pray mindfully and sincerely, al-Khadir tells him a story, a concoction of words, served in the crystal chalice to the thirsty mind, elixir for the soul. This ambrosia comes to us from the dimmest, deepest recesses of our psyche and casts its illuminating, awakening light into the umbra of the ocean that is our unconscious mind.

The story within the story in his dream allows Jalammudin to experience his condition consciously, objectively, as in a mirror. Dream, which is the bridge from our shallow, conscious mind states to the unconscious ones, is water into which we dive to find and bring to the surface pearls of wisdom central to survival, and beautiful beyond description.

The character in the story in Jalammudin's dream within a dream is depressive and suicidal. Who wouldn't be suicidal, deprived of the very water of life? Like Jalammudin, he is in a prison of his own making, a prison of the senses, a jail of doubt. He is thirsty, though the water for his parched soul flows at his feet. The sound of this water torments him like the absence of a beloved torments the lover in his safe, secure, walled-up and walled-in life. The bricks of the prison are our resistance to all things spiritual. Our resistance is the symptom of a world that doesn't endorse spirituality; on the contrary, it discourages and derides it while upholding and extolling, as Iblis does, the god of reason and doubt. In addition, what we are encouraged to worship are the values and norms of social status, fame, power, money, and objects we can buy with money to fill the temples of consumerism that our homes have become. We have allowed ourselves to remain passively obedient to these norms.

But the character in al-Khadir's story within Jalammudin's dream obeys the guide. His conviction and discipline give him the strength to tear off the mortared bricks of his prison one by one and cast them down. With each brick he wrenches and throws down, the sound of the water comes closer till he frees himself and rises anew from the corpse of his old self.

Prayer is the key to resurrection. As soon as Jalammudin whispers the name of his Beloved, the holy name of his glorious God, the chains, shackles, and lock fall away from him. He awakens. It is morning and the world is transformed. His senses—instruments and handmaidens of his soul—see beauty and color, feel and hear the breeze that, like water, flows everywhere. "Wings are restored to the bird whose plumes were torn away," and Jalammudin is free.

CHAPTER 6

MOSES LEARNS
A LESSON

While traveling in the wilderness one early morning, Moses heard the sound of a soulful flute coming from the rolling hills ahead of him. He followed its sound, and came upon a valley. In it he saw a youthful goatherd dancing nimbly and playing his flute with his goats in a beautiful grove of olive trees. The clear shapes of the lichen-covered boulders, the dark and gnarled bark of the trees with their crisp leaves rustling softly in the breeze, the clear outlines of the goats with their curled horns, and the form of the barefooted goatherd with his shining, curly hair that fell to his shoulders and a tunic that reached his knees, was such a brilliant and heartwarming picture that Moses sat and watched for a while.

Moses saw the goatherd put his flute aside, drop to his knees in impassioned prayer, and say:

"O God, where are you? Show yourself to me! Come, my Beloved, reveal yourself to my eyes. I will be your slave. When you awake in the morning, I will bring you fresh milk, warm and foaming from my goats' udders. I will bathe you, wash your hair with water from the cool streams in the summer, and in the winter collect firewood to heat your bathwater. I will comb your hair gently, get rid of the snarls, pick the lice as you sit in the sun and warm your bones, and after cooking you a meal with freshly ground corn flour and freshly picked olives and greens, I will sew your shoes, darn your socks, mend your clothes, and sweep your room. And when you let me, I will rub your feet and kiss your hand. O ecstasy! O God, Friend, Beloved, you to whom I speak in my heart from morning till night, to whom I tell all my sorrows and my joys, and to whom I and all my goats are a sacrifice, tell me, O tell me, where are you?"

"Fool!" cried Moses, approaching him and hitting him with his staff. "Who are you talking to?"

The goatherd was startled, and seeing the powerful presence of the sage before him, he fell at Moses's feet.

"To the one who created me, my goats, these shrubs, my eyes, and light to see it all; to the one who gave me hands to work, and a nose to smell the roses; to the one who is my companion in this wilderness and who my heart seeks through all its sorrows and bewilderment."

"You speak like a fool and a nonbeliever!" Moses yelled at him. "What babble is this? What blasphemy and raving? Your words smell of dung and decay. You have turned the silk robe of faith to rags! Does God have a mouth to drink your milk? Does God have a head with lice in it? Feet? Shoes? Is God your old and poor uncle who needs looking after? Only he who lives and dies needs food and tending. Get up, idiot, and amend your thinking!"

The light went out of the goatherd's eyes at Moses's words. His shoulders slumped in grief and anguish and the landscape turned to endless vistas of sand with only the thin lines of dunes in the distance. He felt his entire world dissolving.

Having chastised the ignorant goatherd, Moses continued on his way. He hadn't gone far when he heard God's voice thundering in his ears.

"Moses! Did you come as a prophet to unite or to break? You have parted my servant from me, and torn our hearts asunder."

"But . . . how could I have done that? I only spoke your truth. Humans limit you, Lord, by creating you in their own images."

"I have bestowed on everyone a way of believing and worshipping according to his understanding and temperament. What do I gain from worship? Nothing! Praying and worship is a kindness I have bestowed on my creatures so they may be tied to me with chords of love. The Hindu worships me in his own way, and the Jew in his. Let them pray any way they know. He who loves me is true to me! Do not seek rules or methods of worship, but love me however you can!"

When Moses heard these reproaches from God, he was stunned. God had just contradicted him, and God was always right. Confused, but always obedient to God's command, Moses ran down the hill to find the goatherd. But the olive grove was empty of goats and goatherd, of song or flute. Moses found the footprints of the goatherd, and followed them hurriedly. Moses knew they were the goatherd's footprints, because the footprints of a bewildered, distraught man are different from the footsteps of those who are certain and sure. Sometimes they are one step ahead of the other, sometimes crisscrossing like the steps of a drunken man tottering in despair, and sometimes smudged, like the flopping belly of a fish on sand in search of water.

The goatherd had gone a long way in his distracted state, and

Moses had to climb a steep hill to find him. Finally Moses saw him by a craggy, harsh, jagged cliff, bare of vegetation. The goatherd was leaning on a staff, and his flock was nowhere in sight. Even the sheep had given up at this height.

"Word has come!" Moses shouted to him as he climbed after him. "Word has come from God, O goatherd! Forgive me! Divine nature is intimate with human nature. Keep the fire of love raging in your soul. Say whatever your distressed heart desires, and give up rules and methods of worship. You are saved, and a whole world along with you. Come, come, return to your grove and your sheep, and worship God as you will!"

When the goatherd turned his face to him, Moses saw that he was no longer youthful. He had aged a lifetime, and the longing that had no name ravaged his countenance. There were vast distances and depths in his eyes that made any witness to them wheel about in infinite spaces with not a form or shape in sight.

"O Moses," the goatherd said in a deep and haunting voice. "I have passed beyond what I imagined. I have journeyed a hundred thousand years on the other side. Your staff prodded me, and the horse of my body at first shied away, then bounded beyond the sky. I am full of gratitude to you. A thousand blessings upon your hand and rod for hitting me! I understand now that when I see an image in a mirror, it is my own image. Words and images no longer matter. Only silence. Only prayer."

He bowed to Moses, then turned and moved steadfastly toward the veiled summits of the mountains before him.

———— ✿ ————

How private prayer is. We meet in congregations on Sundays or Fridays, or whatever other day we deem holy to pray communally with like-minded people. This binds the community, and a few lucky ones even plug into the true reason for the gathering. But very often it is an empty ritual, a habit, a thing to do. The space where we commune with the godhead is fortified, sacred, and silent. Here, in this private space, we can "sleep naked" with the Adored One, speak whatever we like, however we like, pour out our hearts and our minds. We cannot do this, of course, till we first take the leap of faith and trust, and hold sacred the space within ourselves where we commune with God, our Friend, Companion, Master, Mistress, Lord and Lady of Breath.

We cannot share this space with anyone. Speaking or writing about it profanes it. This space is reserved just for the two who are, here, One.

For the goatherd in this story the external setting of prayer is nature, its beauty, privacy, and solitude. As a goatherd, this place is everywhere for him. He plays music to his Beloved and offers to serve him in the best and only way he knows how. He has personified the Invisible God, made him in his own image, and responds to him as he would to a human being with whom he has an intimate relationship.

Moses, the guide who knows that God is formless, sheer energy, Mystery unimaginable, unnameable, beyond images and personifications, stumbles into the goatherd's private space. Instead of seeing or feeling the goatherd's adoration, he gets angry at the goatherd's small-minded image of the godhead. Moses, like most of our guides, is an iconoclast, a breaker of images because he knows that images and idols are too small to contain the Godhood. Moses cannot tolerate the very human need to make the divine as small as we are in order to access and love It. Moses, who sees the goatherd's relationship to the godhead as a pagan practice, lashes out at him with his staff, and proceeds to berate him to correct his thinking and expand his concept of God.

The goatherd's world collapses and his worldview lies in shards about him. His sweet innocence, which Moses terms ignorance, is gone. And from one perspective, it is indeed ignorance. If we take our conceptualizations of the Mystery too seriously, mistake the symbol for the thing itself—a stone, a statue, a golden calf for the Invisible, Formless One with innumerable forms—we are doing It a disservice. Moreover, it can be dangerous because this can and does cause wars between those who have different symbols for the same thing.

But we are creatures of the senses; we need to *personalize* the godhead in order to access It, to hold It in our embrace, near our very physical hearts; we need to give the Mystery names, call it "Beloved," make It as tangible as our sensory needs cry out for. We humans almost *have to* personalize the Mystery. Who can embrace the abstract? And to feed our needs, the Mystery descends to our level to uplift us, give us the gift of all gifts: love.

Both the goatherd and Moses have to learn lessons in this story. Moses has to understand that the divine is very open, malleable, forgiving, accommodating to human need, fluid, and shape-shifting in order to conform to our longing. It is within easy reach for all who turn to It, available to every level of understanding and sensibility, pervious even to "ignorance"; God is not a tyrant demanding obedience to rules, finicky about manners of worship, not a bureaucrat with a list of regulations, but the Arch Lover, waiting, ever waiting, and ready for us to turn to Him even for an instant of utter attention and love. The longing is mutual, Moses is told. Ah, how much more than this do we ever need to know! Is this not the only knowledge, the only truth, sustenance, fulfillment for our hungry hearts?

And to what heights is the goatherd who has adored his Beloved climbing? He is making the journey to the point where even his winged imagination fails, to the vast formless, immeasurable, boundless, infinite, unfathomable Mystery, Force, Power that has brought this whole thing we call our world, ourselves, our universe, into being. Once the goatherd has seen the face of this Mystery (how dependent we are on form, words, images, metaphors, face, body, hands, pronouns, language!), he will never forget that his Beloved, even though he may worship him as being closer than his breath, exceeds his conceptions and language, his very comprehension.

The goatherd is on his way to knowing that he knows nothing about the Mystery that he has condensed into a single image. He will learn at every point in his worship to expand more and more into the Mystery that cannot be congealed into any symbol. He will come to realize, in the poet Percy Bysshe Shelley's words, that "The deep truth is imageless."

And when he does return—for who can inhabit those heights?—and worship, he will remember every time he stumbles upon a certainty, or a judgment based upon it, that it is only his own limitations that limit the godhead.

Being but human, the goatherd will return again and again to a personal Being, one who listens, who is nearer to him than his knowing. He will know only that the Mystery is so contradictory and paradoxical that it is at once personal and impersonal, and that he, our goatherd, is free, as we all are, to range between the two. He will remember when he is inclined to hold on to his version of his Beloved too tightly that this reflects his own limitation and smallness, rather than the Beloved's. As the guide he is on his way to becoming, he will know that though our humanness wants to make the Beloved available to the senses through symbols—we kiss our crosses, adorn our holy books, bow in the direction of our houses of God—He (both He and She and neither) is houseless, and in every direction at once. The goatherd will endeavor to remind himself again and again that he knows nothing, that our concepts and idols are only conveniences that serve as reminders of the Mystery beyond and within us.

CHAPTER 7

THE JUG OF WATER

In a village in the middle of the hot and arid desert lived an old Bedouin, Khalif, and his wife, Aziza. One night, while going to bed after the day's business, Aziza said to her husband:

"The whole world is happy except us. We are the poorest of the poor. There is no bread in the house, we catch and eat gnats, our only sauce is anguish and envy, and our only drink, tears. We don't even possess rags! The burning sunshine of the desert clothes us, and moonlight is our blanket at night. I swear that if a wandering guest comes here tonight, I will steal even his tattered tunic as he sleeps."

"What is left of our life, beloved, that we should cause ourselves so much misery over what we don't have?" Khalif asked. "We are neither beautiful now nor young. Our hair is gray, our skins wrinkled, and our bodies moving toward that great nothing from which we came. Are we going to spend the rest of this fleeting life pursuing wealth? Let us live patiently in wisdom's embrace. Rich life or poor—neither endures. The wise do not attach themselves to the ups and downs of life, but stay above them."

"Ups? When have we known any ups? Wisdom is all very well, dear, for those whose bellies are full," Aziza said, with a sting in her voice. "But we are so poor that all our relatives and acquaintances have fled for fear I may ask them for a handful of lentils. The shop-keepers close their doors when they see me coming."

"You should ask God, instead of relatives and neighbors."

"God! Where is God?"

"Be content with your life, Aziza."

"You call this a life? Especially now as we age, we need some comfort and solace!"

"Stop complaining for a moment and listen, beloved," Khalif replied. "The dove on the tree utters thanks to God even though she doesn't know if there's going to be any food tomorrow. The nightingale sings, trusting in her daily bread. We ought to stop complaining, and pray for our desires to end."

"Desires!" scoffed Aziza, hitting her belly with her fist. "I'll tell you what my desires would be: a roof to protect us, a goat to give us milk . . . milk!" she said, licking her dry lips. "Jars full of lentils, rice, couscous' healthy, fragrant herbs and spices; a dress, good Lord, what joy to have a dress with no holes in it! A bangle of colored glass on my wrist, a small rug for the floor . . . oh, even an iota more than just bare subsistence and animal need, a little bit of delight, of something that feeds my eye as well as my belly! I dare not even dream about desires!"

"These small sorrows are sent to us to test us, beloved. If we don't accept them, our lives will be poisoned. But if we accept them, then our whole life will be made sweet."

"Sweet!" cried Aziza.

"A husband and a wife are like a pair of shoes, Aziza. If one of the shoes is too tight, then both are useless to walk The Way.

We have to give up our ego and anger. I want to march with a stout heart toward contentment and gratitude. Come, walk by my side."

"Contentment! You grab and eat locusts! You fight with dogs on the street for a bone! Haven't I seen you? All this talk of spiritual poverty is empty . . . posturing! Pomposity! Hypocrisy!"

"O woman, how little spiritual understanding you have! How little wisdom in your pea-size brain! But what shall I expect from you? You are only a woman, beyond any reasoning, made entirely of flesh and no spirit!"

"And where is your patience and wisdom when you spring upon your wife like a wild wolf just because she's asking for a few little things to make life a little easier in her old age?"

"I regret the day I was mismatched with you!" Khalif shouted.

"And I with you, you disgrace to Arabs!"

"Materialist! All you can ever think of is money, money, money. Things, things, things!"

"Food, idiot! Food! *Food!*"

"I am sick of you! You are like a jug full of vinegar! In talking to you about spiritual things I am casting pearls before swine. Be silent, or I will leave this house and you in the morning!"

"House! You call this leaky, roofless thing a house? Fine, if you can't support me in these small matters, leave!"

Aziza and Khalif turned their backs to each other on their broken cot propped up with stones and mended with rags, but neither of them slept after their quarrel. Aziza tried through the night to imagine a life without Khalif, and was filled with desolation. For the first time in a long, long time, she prayed—not that her desires be eliminated, but fulfilled.

Khalif, too, was more disturbed than he would admit. Many thoughts jostled in his head. Seeing himself reflected in his wife's reminders of his own hungers, he was ashamed at the discovery that he was not as spiritually evolved as he had hoped. If he had been, would he have judged her for what he himself felt beneath his spiritual hypocrisy? He was not as content as he had hoped; he had not transcended his human needs. How ashamed he was of his lack of self-knowledge and control; how he had failed to examine his own heart and therefore be more compassionate with his wife.

In the morning, while Khalif was reluctantly packing a bag and looking for a way out of his threat to leave home, Aziza threw herself at his feet, wept, and pleaded with him to stay.

"Without you, my beloved, the treasures of the world would mean nothing to me."

Khalif's heart melted like wax in fire when he heard these words. He lifted her up and embraced her.

"Forgive me. I'm so sorry and so ashamed at my harsh words; you were right to point out my shortcomings, to goad me into intro-spection. You are the life of my soul, Aziza. I want to make you happy but don't know how."

"I prayed last night and Allah sent me a wonderful thought! Go to the great, the merciful and generous Sultan of Baghdad. That great king will make you a king."

"What a happy, hopeful thought, Aziza! But . . ." He paused agitatedly. "How can I go empty-handed to the king? What gift can I take him? We have nothing! And will he even consent to see a beggar like me?"

"Don't panic, my love. We have something that even the richest of kings don't have. This," she said, bringing down a jug with five spouts from a shelf.

"Oh," he cried in relief. "I had forgotten all about it!"

"When you live in the desert, there is nothing more precious than this!" Aziza said, with a sparkle in her eyes.

"Sew up the jug in felt so that I may not spill it on the way, and the king may break his fast with our gift."

Aziza did so, and warning Khalif to keep the jug safe from highwaymen and boys throwing stones, she bid him goodbye as he began his journey to Baghdad.

After a long, hot, wearying journey through the desert, during which he kept the jug safe, Khalif arrived at the gate of the king in Baghdad. Surrounding the palace were magnificent rose gardens and tree-lined meandering streams. All around the gate Khalif saw crowds of petitioners, some carrying expensive gifts of gold for the king in the hope that he would fulfill their desires. They came from high and low, sheikhs and beggars waiting their turn. As some waited, others carried away loads of treasures and robes of honor.

And as Khalif stood there, ashamed of his jug sewn in a green rag, the sultan's officers motioned to him. Khalif turned around to see if they were calling someone else, but when he turned around, they were standing by him.

"Come! Come!" they said warmly. "Bounty seeks beggars as much as beggars seek bounty!" And while Khalif stood there feeling shabby, they took him to the baths, bathed him in warm water with attar, rose water, and jasmines, and then rubbed him down with almond oil. They clothed him in new garments that were soft and smooth against his skin. They made him a bed of silken sheets to rest upon, and before they left, Khalif gave them the jug to give to their king.

"Give this to the kind sultan, so he may redeem his humble servant from poverty. It's sweet water. My wife collected this precious water from a ditch. And be careful with it. It's fragile, and I have carried it carefully a long, long way," Khalif said.

The officers smiled, and humbly accepted the jug as though it contained a rare elixir, for when you serve a great master, his qualities rub off on you.

Before falling asleep, Khalif rubbed his hands on the soft silk sheets. He thought of Aziza, of how pleased she would be with such luxury. Yes, he wanted to see her happy, and hoped the king would fulfill their desires to have enough for their needs.

Early in the morning, the officers took the jug to the sultan. He had just woken up when they presented the jug to him. When he heard the story, he took the jug in his hands and said to his smiling officers, "He brought me his most prized possession. How rare and beautiful this gift is!" Then he poured the dirty ditch water into a crystal chalice, and quaffed it, to the amazement of his courtiers.

The sultan smacked his lips, as if it were the tastiest of wines, and said to his officers, "Go, fill this jug with gold and gems, and return it to the Bedouin. And give him a robe of honor. And because he came to us the long way, through the desert, let him return the shorter way, by water. Make sure you see him home."

When Khalif awoke, his jug, filled with gems, and a robe of honor were waiting for him in handsome traveling cases. He was in a daze, as if in a dream, as they mounted him on a horse and took him to the Tigris River.

Riding through the street on a well-caparisoned horse, Khalif was proud, both of himself and of his wife, whose desires had sent him thither to such a generous king. Just being in the same town as the king had filled Khalif with a sense of well-being. He realized that his wife, with her material desires, and he, with his spiritual ones, were like the two wings which enable a bird to fly to paradise. How happy she would be at his return with all this wealth!

Dismounting on the banks of the river, Khalif stood amazed and stunned. He had never, ever seen so much crystal-clear water in his life, flowing by in endless, inexhaustible currents. Its expanse was so huge that large boats and barges with fishing nets bobbed upon it, and its bed was strewn with pearls and precious stones.

And suddenly Khalif felt very ashamed. To have given such a king a jug of dirty water! Oh, what must he have thought! And oh, what utter generosity to return his piteous gift with pearls!

He turned to the officers in a state of agitation, but their smiles reassured him.

"He broke his fast with the water from your jug," they told him.

Khalif dropped to the ground and wept.

"Arise, Bedouin, and rejoice," they said. "Here, everyone who comes with a desire is welcome. And each receives according to his request. Those who come for bread receive bread and other viands. Those seeking material goods receive bags of gold, and those who seek Truth reach the Sea."

As Khalif stepped into a barge that was all decked out with a beautiful canopy, in which sat four men with paddles, his heart sank suddenly, and his eyes welled up with tears. Like an ass he had gone to the sultan to beg for straw! Why, oh why had he not asked to be given the gift of all gifts, that unseen rose garden beneath which Kawthar, the river of paradise, flows, and on whose banks the saints, freed of all human desire, and anchored firmly in the eternal world, roam in leisure and in joy? Why had he not asked for the Truth, and reached the Sea?

"Knock, knock on the door of Reality, Bedouin!" one of the rowers said to Khalif. "And know that it will be opened to you!"

The words rang in Khalif's ears, reassuring him that nothing was lost. Watching the play of light upon the waves of the water that carried him home to his beloved wife, he knew in his heart that the very proximity of the sultan had set him on The Way: The river would eventually carry him to the Sea.

———— ✤ ————

In "The Jug of Water," Rumi redeems the feminine, and in doing so, redeems himself from being labeled a misogynist. Though Aziza at first appears to be another nag and shrew, she avoids a bitter destiny by turning to love and trust. In fact, she vindicates women and shows us how to live in all our humanity *and* divinity.

Like all shrewish women, Aziza is discontent with her life. She's tired of living in extreme poverty and disappointed in her husband's reluctance to do what it takes to provide for them. She lives in a time when women had to rely on their husbands to provide. If they could have worked, earned, bought what they needed and wanted, or undertaken a long, hard, and dangerous journey through a desert to visit a sultan, it seems, based on the spirit she shows in the beginning of the story, Aziza would have.

And what does she want? A new roof, a goat, a stocked larder, a new dress, bangles, a rug. How human and adorable she is in her desires!

Khalif, on the other hand, is typical of the man who lives in his head, with ideas and ideals that are unrealistic and hypocritical. He mouths spiritual platitudes, has an answer for the sublimation of each of his wife's needs, and possesses a precarious wisdom. His sour-grapes philosophy is ballasted with a grasping hunger that makes him grab and eat locusts and fight with dogs for bones. Rather than confronting and admitting his needs, he reprimands himself for having them. Regret and self-abasement is another form of ego in which we think that we are being spiritual by depriving ourselves and suppressing our legitimate desires.

Khalif is dismissive of his wife's materialistic nature as just another indication of women's inability to rise above flesh. Why deride flesh, Guru Nanak asks. We are *of* flesh. Matter is on a continuum with spirit; the two are tied with a ligature, two notes that are a single phrase. A little bit of desire, not the sort that plunges us down the slippery slope of constant craving, is a part of need. No one knows it better than the Creatrix who has planted it in our hearts. As Kabir sings in one of his shabads, "If we don't ask the Giver, whom are we going to ask?" Even the richest of the rich are beggars at your door, he says. He has no qualms about saying bluntly to God: "Here, take back your prayer beads; I cannot worship you while I am hungry. Give me flour, ghee, salt, a pound of beans, a bed, a mattress, a quilt. Satisfied, I will worship you with love. This is not greed." He ends, "Your name shall be my ornament."

Most of the ten Sikh gurus lived well and encouraged their followers to engage in commerce, not obsessively, but in a detached way. They made it clear in the many hymns in the Sikh holy book, from which I take this song of Kabir's, that life is meant to be lived to its fullest, that we can only do so when we love the Beloved, source of all material and spiritual satisfaction. Neither do Jews believe that reality is only spiritual, or that matter is only an illusion. Jane Austen illustrates this philosophy as well in *Emma*: "A very narrow income has a tendency to contract the mind, and sour the temper. Those who can barely live, and who live perforce in a very small, and generally very inferior, society, may well be illiberal and cross."

In goading her husband to strive for material fulfillment,

Aziza discovers her own capacity for humility, love, and spiritual strength. In exposing to Khalif his own hypocrisy, she provokes him to examine his life, a prerequisite for embarking on The Way. His first realization after their fight is "Maybe I'm not as spiritual as I think I am." And Aziza's realization is that without her husband and love, all the treasure in the world would be worthless. This is the moment she transforms from a shrew to a woman who is whole and balanced.

My mother was both like and unlike Aziza. Because she had been too damaged during a prolonged period after her marriage at the age of sixteen, when she was badly mistreated by her mother-in-law without my father's intervention, she lacked Aziza's humble lovingness. This kept her on the path of shrewishness. But like Aziza, her desire for material comfort and plenty and her spiritual trust kept her husband on The Way, where spirituality did not exclude materiality. My father lost his wealthy father at the age of two, and the subsequent poverty of his family turned him to the Mystery for emotional comfort, and to a determination to uplift his family materially.

Just one incident will suffice as an example of my mother's trust before I return to Aziza and Khalif's story. After my father retired at an early age from the military, where he reached the rank of brigadier, he was very troubled by the fact that he owned no home and had three children to marry, which in India is an expensive affair. My brother told my parents flat out that if Mother kept spending the way she habitually did, loving all sorts of material things, they were not to come asking him for anything. My mother was very agitated by this because she felt her son had no business telling her what to do, and cried and prayed herself to sleep. Like Aziza, she did not pray for her desires to be eliminated but for them to be fulfilled. That night she dreamt that the tenth Sikh guru, Guru Gobind Singh, was standing next to a man shoveling coal and saying, "*Dhan kola dhan kola*" ("Blessed coal, blessed coal"). A few days later, my father was allotted a gas station, chosen out of 5,000 applicants. The connection between coal and petroleum was revealed. It was a lucrative business and my mother was able to build the house of her dreams and continue to spend freely, not excessively, on the things she felt she wanted and needed.

Only the austere guide, for whom I personally have no use, discourages us from enjoying life in all its materiality. Though many Sufis extol poverty, Rumi is obviously rooting for Aziza in this story.

I used to believe, and still do, with some modifications, that the purpose of prayer is to ask not for this or that material advantage, but for *qualities* like courage, understanding, the ability and humility to see the truth of oneself, for endurance to withstand whatever life throws our way. I still think this is a superior form of prayer, but I believe, too, that we can turn to the divine for *all* our needs.

I learned an important lesson about prayer one recent New Year's Day. I had gone many days with a lock through my lips that kept me from drinking at the holy font of prayer. Exhausted beyond description from a very challenging year, I had fallen, like Jalammudin, into a dark stream of negative thoughts. Instead of praying, I turned to the Invisible Being with whom my soul is in constant dialogue, not in humility but in shrewish pique, in demands and reproaches. "Are you going to send me another avalanche? How much more are you going to heap on me? When will this be over? Death is preferable to this!" Fool that I am, forgetful and unaware, I didn't realize I was only perpetuating my suffering. Before going to bed, on the verge of what I felt was an emotional breakdown, something in me mercifully made me turn to the Friend with the simple and humble supplication "Help me."

In an instant my locks and chains fell away and, like Jalammudin, I slept.

After her initial outburst at fate and her husband (which of us wouldn't feel anger at dire poverty?), Aziza feels no sense of entitlement; no resentment at her lot, for not having been given what most humans have; she feels no anger and makes no demands. She simply prays for help and gets it. That is what prayer does: It relaxes us, takes away our anxiety, gives us that peace in which our hearts and brains flow like water in new channels, broadening our vision, changing our perspective from despair to hope. It gives us a direction: Go to the generous and merciful Sultan of Baghdad.

Khalif's unwillingness to go empty-handed to the sultan prompts Aziza to part with their most precious possession, the jug with five spouts filled with life-sustaining water.

What is this jug with five spouts? I didn't know the answer when I wrote the story, seven or eight years ago. I have visited many a museum and read many books to find it. It does not exist. It is only now that I have an inkling of what it might mean. Rumi meant it to symbolize the human body. Five spouts, five senses? And what is the only gift truly worth giving to the Beloved? Our bodies, our lives, given to us, loaned if you will, must be surrendered voluntarily and joyfully to the rightful owner. What the couple is surrendering to the sultan is nothing less than their whole being.

Who can resist this, let alone the Creator whose one desire is, like the roots of all our desires, to be loved? The sultan does not want prayers. Like He tells Moses, He wants us to bind ourselves to him with chords of love. He wants only our heart burning for union. In exchange for a morsel of our love, for our heartfelt gift of dirty ditch water, he wants only to give bountifully. It is only in this surrender that all manner of wealth and wisdom becomes possible. Everything in us becomes pure with this surrendering. Those of us who fear that this jug is filled with dirty water collected from a ditch will be heartened by the tiding that the Sultan of All Sultans is so pleased with this gift that He pours it into His crystal chalice and drinks it as if it were the rarest of elixirs.

When our surrender is heartfelt, then we can ask for anything. If our love is only for show, only a front for our wanting and craving, then our asking is nothing but cleverness and greed.

Aziza's desire is based in faith that the Sultan of Baghdad *can* fill her begging bowl to overflowing. Her faith fulfills her, shows us a way of being in the world with an embodied, fleshed-out wisdom, and starts Khalif on his journey to himself, which is, after all, the journey to the Ocean of Being. He develops, through the love for his wife, true introspection and openness to the divine; from an empty windbag he becomes a man of substance. He begins. And on this journey, the beginning is everything. Once he has begun, Khalif knows that if he persists with devotion on his path, The Way itself will carry him on its back, like a river, to his destination—the Ocean, our origin and destination, giver and quencher of our desires.

Khalif also learns that matter and spirit are not separate. He becomes aware, as Rumi says, that "his wife with her material desires and he with his spiritual ones are like the two wings which enable a bird to fly to paradise."

Often it is desire for something that sends us to the Court of the Sultan. We go for gain and come away with the gift of The Way, the provisions, mental and physical, to stay on it to the very end—the emptying of the rivers we are into the Unseen Sea.

———— ❀ ————

CHAPTER 8

THE DARK FLOWER
OF JUSTICE

Everyone thought Nasirrudin, a young man without any kin, was very lazy. He made no pretense of his secret desire to make money without having to work for it.

"O God," he would pray, "give me riches without labor! It is you who have made me the way I am! I am sluggish and easily fatigued by the world's many requirements. I cannot bear the burdens of bosses and jobs. I like to move slowly through my day without any concern for time, praying and reading, studying, resting, contemplating, and reflecting. Surely you who provide for people such as me can send me wealth that I might live in comfort and plenty, without any worries and hunger! Or at least, Lord, send me my daily bread. O King of Kings, you who provide sustenance to the embryo in the womb, fulfill my desire!"

People who were living by the sweat of their brows would speak derisively of Nasirrudin and think him very foolish, if not stupid. They were neither kind nor generous to him, so he was always hungry.

"God has provided you with a means of fulfilling your need, you scoundrel: Use your hands and your feet and your mind!" they would say to him. Nevertheless, despite their ridicule and rudeness, Nasirrudin continued to trust in Providence's power to provide for him, and to pray for the fulfillment of his longing.

One morning, as he was praying fervently, somebody banged on his door with a great rattling, broke the bolt and the latch, and entered his room. It was a beautiful, fat cow with large horns, and Nasirrudin jumped up from his prayers, grabbed a rope, bound her feet with it, and, without any qualms or mercy, slit her throat. Once she lay dead upon the floor, Nasirrudin went to fetch the butcher so he might help him rip off her beautiful hide. He would now have meat and money for a good while!

But the butcher knew the owner of the cow, Hamza, who arrived, enraged, at Nasirrudin's door and yelled obscenities at him. "Return my cow, or pay me the price. Now!" he yelled.

"It's mine, and has been sent to me as an answer to my prayers," Nasirrudin replied. "The cow is not yours but a gift to me from God! Why else would she break open my door and enter my room this way?"

The owner of the cow was enraged beyond words. He caught Nasirrudin by his collar and proceeded to beat him black and blue. Then he threw him on his donkey and took him to King David, known far and wide for his impeccable justice.

Hamza bowed to David. "Please bestow some sense and intelligence onto this criminal and impostor, Your Majesty. My cow ran into his yard and his room, and he killed her! He can't revive her, and he won't pay me her worth! There is no doubt about where justice lies in this case! He's a lazy good-for-nothing, doesn't believe in labor, and lives off the sweat of others. Give me justice, my lord."

"And what do you have to say, young man?" David asked, looking into the eyes of the disheveled young man in a tattered cloak.

"I labor a great deal in my supplications, Your Majesty," Nasirrudin replied. "The cow came to me in answer to my prayers."

"O good people! Gather around and hear his drivel!" Hamza cried.

"The owner of the cow is right!" they all yelled. "Replace the cow, pay up, or go to prison!"

Nasirrudin shut his eyes and prayed: "O you who have put these prayers on my tongue and in my heart, and raised my hopes, shield me, protect me from their wrath, even if I have erred."

"Well? Speak, noble one," David said to Nasirrudin.

The audience gasped. Noble! This lout noble?!

"Why did you destroy the property of this honorable man?" David asked.

"Like Joseph, I am a dreamer, my lord. Fate has thrust me into a deep dungeon and I escape it through my dreams. God is my friend in this dungeon. I pray to Him, plead with Him night and day to send me a livelihood that is lawful."

"Lawful!" screamed the crowd. "What's lawful about killing another's cow?"

"I killed her so that I might give alms in thankfulness to Him who knows unseen things and answers prayers," Nasirrudin replied.

"Tell me," asked David, addressing Nasirrudin, "did anyone give you this cow? Did you buy or inherit her? If not, you have performed an illegal act. If you haven't farmed, how do you expect to reap what you haven't sown? Go pay this good man his due. Borrow if you must, and labor away your dues."

"Long live our just and fair king, David!" the crowd shouted, as they surrounded Nasirrudin, ready to take him to prison if he did not make amends.

Nasirrudin lamented and wept in his heart. "Cast your light into David's heart, O Lord! Spare me the torture of life in prison, or, what is worse, a life of drudgery," he prayed.

As David turned to leave, something about Nasirrudin's face rapt in prayer moved him deeply.

"Listen," David said, holding up his hand to the crowd. "Let the young man go. I need a day so I may go into a solitary place and seek advice from the Knower of Mysteries. Meditation opens a window through which the sunshine of grace pours upon me and shows me The Way."

Certain that the question of justice in this case was as clear as day, the crowd dispersed while David set off for the place where he would lock his doors and be entirely alone with Him, who was closer to him than his jugular vein.

The next day all the litigants returned to court, and noisily awaited David's judgment. They fell silent as David entered the hall.

The king looked at the plaintiff and said, "Demand justice only if you deserve justice. Give up your claim to the cow, Hamza. Go home, and live in peace. If you refuse to do this, a worse fate will befall you."

Hamza and the crowd were in an uproar. "King David has lost his mind," they muttered. And then loudly they demanded justice and an explanation for this absurd judgment.

"I'm warning you, Hamza. Shut your eyes and look within yourself for the answer. If you find yourself utterly blameless, then we shall speak of justice."

"What have I ever done to deserve this?" Hamza shouted. "It's all as clear as the nose on my face!"

Hamza's speech incited the crowd to anger.

"Silence!" David said. "You have not taken my advice to go

home and live in peace. So now I say, Hamza, give this young man, Nasirrudin, all your wealth: all your cows, and all your camels. If not, you shall fare even worse than this."

"Insult to injury!" cried Hamza, pulling out his hair. "Listen, O people, the wise king has become a fool!"

"Your children and your wife are also now Nasirrudin's slaves. Even now, O unconscious man, incapable of introspecting and remembering your crimes, go home and live in peace!"

But David's words only put Hamza in a crazy frenzy, tearing at his garments, running from end to end of the hall, glaring with rolling eyes at the king, and screaming,

"Hark ye, hark ye, the time of injustice has come!"

"O king!" the people shouted. "This is unworthy of you! How can you treat an innocent man thus? What faith will we have in you after this manifestly unjust judgment?"

"Come, all, let us get to the root of this issue. Come, bring shovels and follow me! But tie up this criminal, Hamza, so he doesn't escape from justice," King David said.

Bewildered and curious, the crowd, with Hamza bound hand and foot in chains, followed David to the outskirts of the town, where in a plane field stood a huge tree with wide spreading branches. David paused beneath it, and pointed to dark red flowers by the trunk of the tree.

"You demand the law. Here it is. You want to confess, Hamza?"

"To what? To what must I confess?" Hamza spat.

"O unreflecting man! You, you killed Nasirrudin's grandfather, and his only son, Nasirrudin's father, and buried them here."

Hamza strained against his chains while the crowd shouted, "What evidence do we have of this dastardly allegation?"

"What proof, indeed?" Hamza shouted.

"Ask him," David said.

"I did nothing of the sort!" Hamza said indignantly.

"Blood sleeps not, nor forgets. The sown seed shoots up from the loam. Hamza was Nasirrudin's grandfather's slave. After killing Nasirrudin's grandfather and father, this scoundrel abandoned the little orphan grandson, this young man here, and appropriated everything of his master's: wives, slaves, animals, property, and wealth through forged documents."

"But how do we know for sure?" the crowd asked.

"Dig up the earth here and find their skeletons. Nothing can be hidden from God's eye. Here, dig here where these red flowers have grown from the blood."

And sure enough, two skeletons were discovered deep in the earth, together with a knife bearing Hamza's name.

"Evil will out," King David said. "No one can hide from the sight of God. There is a justice greater than ours. This man made a noise about one cow, when he himself took his master's hundred cows and hundred camels. Never once did he supplicate to God, or open his heart to Him. Come, O demander of justice, receive it."

There was no restraining the crowd's fury. Like a wild animal with many hands and feet, it fell upon Hamza and dispatched him with his own knife. The wicked man was killed and King David's subjects henceforth began to look within themselves for answers before judging others, and to supplicate and pray when they were bewildered and lost.

"Come," David said, putting his arm around Nasirrudin's shoulders, and walking back into town. "Enjoy now the fulfillment of the desire placed in you by the mysterious Lord of Justice."

————— ❀ —————

How human Rumi's characters and their stories are! Rumi does not shy away from any part of human nature. Like the Sikh gurus, Rumi affirms without judgment the whole range of our desires; like them he seems to say, pray to the Giver, ask for what your destiny makes you want with a passion that cannot be reasoned with, ask with your entire self, surrender your whole life, desires and all, to the Ocean of Mercy, trust with all your heart, and you *will* get what you ask for.

Some desires are so strong that they are given to us, almost like commands. Like Aziza, whose desire could not be kept at bay, Nasirrudin too asks ceaselessly for comfort and plenty, or at least his daily bread. He is a dreamer who prays for a free and easy ride to riches. He wants money without working so he can be at leisure to do all those important things—study, pray, reflect—that fall by the wayside because of the compelling quotidian.

I understand Nasirrudin's desire very well. I too wanted to be economically self-sufficient without having to earn a livelihood through teaching so that I could have the leisure to write. I was granted my wish, but not, I must admit ungratefully, as immediately as I would have liked. Even though I resonated with Nasirrudin's longing subconsciously, I was appalled at him when I first began to read Rumi's story in the *Mathnawi*. As readers afflicted with the puritanical work ethic, we cannot and do not condone or approve of Nasirrudin's laziness in wanting money without working for it. Hadn't I worked for mine, taken on jobs for what the Indians call "the sake of the stomach"? Nasirrudin lost my sympathy when he slaughtered another's cow. I began to side with the villagers.

And yet, despite my conscious self-righteous stance, like King David I trusted Nasirrudin. Though his fellow men see him as a lazy thief who lives off others' labors, we have to admit that Nasirrudin exudes innocence. There is purity, openness, and honesty in his relationship to the divine. There is no subterfuge in his heart, no lying, no pretense. His supplications are the genuine, heartfelt pleadings of a man of deep faith. He appeals to the Power that has spontaneously generated this desire within him for a reason he does not know.

He knows only that God, from within him, knows everything he feels in all the nooks and crannies of his heart, so why hide anything? He knows the Divine who fashioned him, and to whom he belongs, heart, mind, soul, pocketbook, need, and fantasy, is the One who sends him his desires.

Rumi tests the reader, as he does the villagers. He challenges our certainties and judgments and lets us see the limitations of our opinions. By twisting our heads around, this story shows us, like Socrates, whose wisdom lies in his knowledge that he knows nothing, how blind we are to the vast scheme of things.

The Jewish king David—poet, warrior, singer, author of the lovely Psalms in the Bible—is another image, like the sultan, of the godhead. David is wise because he listens, first to the entire case, to Hamza and Nasirrudin, and then to the voice of his soul that tells him to meditate on the verdict that he has so peremptorily declared. He turns to the Knower of Mysteries for counsel.

When David returns from his retreat, he can see beyond the immediate circumstances. In this story, Rumi gives us a glimpse of the long view of time, of the vaster, cosmic design and arc of our lives, of the unknown, recondite depths and labyrinths of the histories of our souls. These workings seem irrational to our myopic realities. We do not see how we plant the seeds of our future in the present.

Rumi's story tells us that past, present, and future are contiguous on The Way, ongoing in the service of consciousness, lesson learning, and transformation. It lies beyond evidence and far exceeds the narrow beam of our intellects.

We have most to learn from Hamza, the "owner" of the cow. He does not pray. On The Way our greatest and highest form of prayer is introspection. But Hamza remains self-righteous and angry till his last breath, perhaps because he was a slave and is understandably still angry and vengeful about his past. Even so, each one of us, no matter how difficult our lives have been, owes it to ourself to introspect, to see where *we* have gone wrong. Hamza projects all his troubles onto the innocent Nasirrudin instead of searching for the cause within his own life and actions. Not for an instant does he stop long enough to self-examine.

Hamza is our face in the mirror at our worst. We blame others for our troubles. We think the cause of our unhappiness lies in *them*. We blame God for sending us afflictions, having forgotten the cardinal fact of our existence: Our survival testifies to our "sins." Even if we are not Christians who subscribe to the theory of "original sin," let us reflect for a moment on how many beings we have killed, eaten, and destroyed to be here. Destroying and being destroyed is our destiny. None of us are sinless. I think back on how many people I have hurt in my journey to get to this point in time, how many little and big lies I have told, how often I have judged others without judging myself first. We have only to look inside ourselves in the ruthless light of unwavering honesty to see the truth of our own sinfulness, which is not a judgment but a fact. Like Hamza, we have forgotten our own pasts and delude ourselves into thinking we are "good" and "just." When we find ourselves suffering, thrashing about like fish on sand, thinking we have done nothing to deserve it, we do not remember to take responsibility; we do not remember that the universe *is* poetically just. How often do we simply stop in the whirlwind of reproaches and lamentations, and pray to get an insight into our own souls and past behavior?

The simple words, "help me" will not bring aid before we have ripped apart our hearts to see the falsity throbbing there. It is only after we bring our own darkness to consciousness, acknowledge it, that we can surrender it to the Being who has made the universe, and ourselves within it, as it *IS*.

Hamza, whose fate it is to die blind, is too limited in his vision to remember his past. He has no consciousness of his own behavior and does not introspect. If he did, he would have searched his soul to find the cause of his current troubles. Though it may seem to some that in life we can get away with a lot, all our literature—Greek and Shakespearean tragedies, our greatest novels and spiritual stories, our religious and spiritual texts—remind us over and over that we are undoubtedly accountable for our actions. In the words of Job in the Bible, "They that plow iniquity, and sow wickedness, reap the same." The Koran says, "They shall reap the fruit of what they did, and ye of what ye do!" In Guru Nanak's words, we eat what we sow.

That's why the concept of karma in Hinduism, Buddhism, and Sikhism admonishes us to be careful *now*, or we *will* suffer for it in this or our next lives. Even if we don't believe in an afterlife, enough literature and examples from life exist to show us the consequences of the unexamined life in the here and now. Wrongful, prideful, irresponsible thinking, greedy and lustful behavior are their own punishment. They do not promote peace and trouble the minds of even the most criminal of people. We would do well to learn from Hamza's fate.

PART 3

SURRENDER TO THE COSMIC WILL

It beseems the generous
to give money:
But the generosity
of the lover
is surrender
of his soul!

MATHNAWI, Book I, 2235

Do not speak, so the Spirit
May speak for thee:
In the ark of Noah
Leave off swimming!

MATHNAWI, Book III, 1307

CHAPTER 9

THE WITCH OF KABUL

King Kafur of Kabul was given to musing and introspection on the state of his soul and the world. Every event, every dream, every thought and emotion became fodder for reflection and wonder.

One night he dreamt that his son, the prince Tawfiq, the lamp of his life, died suddenly. The king's grief was so intense that even in the dream he came upon the very verge of death. In the convulsion of his death throes he awoke with a start. Realizing his son had died only in a dream, the king was filled with an unbound joy so powerful that he felt he was dying from it. When he recovered sufficiently from the grip of these powerful passions, King Kafur laughed aloud at the folly of man destined to live thus in the troughs and crests of contrary emotions. As he walked in his beautiful garden full of rare flowers, exotic trees, and songbirds, he mused about how malleable and fickle the human mind is, and how easy it is for blind humanity to drown in the illusions of both dream and reality.

But King Kafur's dream made him aware that life is uncertain and perishable. Because he had not yet learned that when the candle of the body begins to perish, one needs to light the candle of the spirit, he resolved to light another lamp with the lamp of his mortal son, Tawfiq: Marry him off so he could beget a son. To this end he began to search his kingdom for a suitable bride.

Meanwhile, in another strand of the story, there lived in Kabul a ninety-year-old hag called Aliya who had never married. She hadn't wanted or needed to. Having been youthful late into her life, and beautiful too, she had had her pick of lovers. But at the age of ninety, when no one would have her, she was extremely lonely and longed to have a man around her. One man in particular had filled her with yearning, and she spent many days dreaming of their union. She longed to have a glamorous wedding. Though her body was falling apart, her heart was young, and her passions still raged. Oh, to dress up as a bride! To wait for her beloved to come to her on the wedding night on a bed strewn with jasmine and rose petals! Oh, to be naked, skin to burning skin, with her lover!

Aliya resolved to fulfill her dreams by whatever means possible.

To this end she began to repair her decrepit body. She went to surgeons to get her sagging breasts uplifted; she applied salves and unguents to her skin, wrinkled like the neck of an old camel; dyes to her hair that had turned white like muddied snow; oils to her bare gums to make her teeth grow back. She got massages to straighten her back, bent like a bow. She plucked her eyebrows, applied rouge to her cheeks, and kohl to her eyes. But all her efforts made her look more haggard, like a dilapidated house whose walls and ceiling had caved, but whose door was painted in loud and garish colors.

When all Aliya's efforts failed, the old crone, who had no spiritual leanings, tried another trick. She had heard about the power of the Koran, but instead of reading it and contemplating its wisdom, she cut off portions of the holy book and stuck them to her face to hide the creases and crevices. But whenever she moved or put on her head scarf, the bits of paper fell off. She put spittle on them and stuck them to her face again. But when she spoke or chewed, they fell off again. She glued them on with firmer glue, and went to the object of her passions, who was none other than King Kafur's son, Prince Tawfiq.

Tawfiq, a good Sufi who lived for the now and paid no heed to tomorrow, on guard against the thousand distractions that waylay humans from moment to moment, saw through Aliya's disguise to her depraved intentions, spurred his horse whenever he saw her on the street, and galloped past her as fast as he could.

Frustrated beyond measure, Aliya called on Iblis—Satan himself—to give her beauty, youth, and wealth with which to ensnare Prince Tawfiq.

"Leave me alone, you foul hag!" Iblis spat as soon as she evoked him.

"Help me!" she screamed.

She was so repulsive that even Iblis began to wax spiritual.

"Scrape off your lusts from the mirror of your heart, you old harlot, and make your cleansed heart your beauty."

But Aliya was persistent in her pleading. Iblis, who was incapable of bestowing either beauty or youth, was eager to rid himself of her. He gave her a vial of glittering dust that would give her the illusion of youth, beauty, and wealth if she sprinkled it on whomever she wanted to enchant. The dust would work only on a person who had momentarily lapsed in his vigilance against the sorcery of the world.

King Kafur, meanwhile, began his search for a bride for Tawfiq. He resolved to find a girl who was poor, but beautiful and virtuous, rather than a haughty and wealthy princess. He found such a girl in a distant corner of his kingdom. She was the daughter of an ascetic, and her beauty and virtue were inexpressible in words. Let it be sufficient to say that she was a union of all that is best and highest in human nature, steady and unwavering on her path to abide by what is true beneath all the glitter and falsity of the world.

Riding his horse on the way to his wedding, the prince passed by Aliya in the narrow streets. Preoccupied with thoughts of his ensuing marriage, he was inattentive when Aliya sprinkled her glittering dust on him, and instantly the prince reined in his horse. Charmed by Aliya's coy laughter, he took one look into the sunken, puffy eyes in her haggard face plastered over with fragments of the Koran, and was smitten beyond remedy. Like a spider, she had caught him in her web and tightened her knots around his heart.

Prince Tawfiq got off his horse and followed the old crone. The world glittered and shimmered all around him. The narrow, dirty streets became winding garden paths; the crumbling houses became palaces; the ankle bells on Aliya's feet as she walked ahead of him were the most enticing of sounds; her cracked and crumbling heels were the most alluring of bodily parts, and the folds of her filthy head scarf the diaphanous veils of a mystery that held the deepest of sensual pleasures.

At the wedding, King Kafur and Tawfiq's bride waited and waited, but Tawfiq did not turn up. After many hours of faithful patience from the wedding party and guests, a messenger finally came and relayed what had happened. Although the steadfast bride did not despair or give up hope, King Kafur was distraught. As if in mourning with the king, all the vegetation in his kingdom and in his garden began to wither and die. Even the songbirds became silent. The king sent many anguished messages to his son to open his eyes to the truth of his enchantment, but the prince was deaf to them all. Tawfiq was not capable of extricating himself from the clutches of the witch, nor did he feel the need to. He was in bliss, bestowing kisses on the soles of the hag's shoes, and staring into her eyes for hours on end. His father was just a doddering old fool with his spiritual mumbo jumbo, the prince thought. Life was for living, and sitting at the feet of his beautiful dark goddess was life. Yes, he was probably trapped, like his father said he was, but what a sweet trap Aliya was! He was not in her "clutches," as his father called it, but in her scintillating embrace.

An entire year passed, in which Tawfiq's wife-to-be waited patiently, with unwavering hope for her beloved. King Kafur despaired for himself and his son, and forgot altogether to muse and contemplate with detachment the state of the human being so prone to delusion and despair. His deep desire for his son to return to The Way and escape seduction by the old hag caused the king immeasurable anguish.

King Kafur eventually found himself standing before the door of death, but unlike in his dream, his peril was real. With one foot already in the door, he awoke suddenly to the realization that instead of judging his son for being in the clutches of the witch, he should have judged himself for being in the clutches of his own despair! He was just as deluded as his son.

He sat down, turned his attention toward the dark labyrinths of his own heart, traveled through them to the abode of his Beloved, and surrendered himself and his son to the Mystery that creates entrapments for unsuspecting humankind.

"You alone, O God, have commanded this to happen. How could anything in the world be without your will?"

King Kafur gave up all attempts to force his son back to The Path, surrendered his own will and wanting to the will of God, and henceforth stayed with soft supplications and prayers.

One day during his prayers, King Kafur looked up and saw in the distance undulating waves of light coming toward him. As they got nearer, a radiant figure emerged from them. The king knew help had arrived from the land of the Invisible. It was a master magician who alone could engage in combat with Iblis's forces on earth, and with Aliya, the crone.

The master magician defeated Aliya after a protracted battle in the tombs of Kabul by using the same delusions as hers, but that is another long story. Suffice it to say she was defeated, and the gnarled knots she had bound around the prince's heart were loosened. The prince's eyes opened, and as he looked at Aliya shorn of all her magic, standing before him with her little bits of paper stuck all over her crumbling face, he was amazed at his bewitchment. He began to be repulsed by himself, but caught himself in time and surrendered his impurity to God, who makes all things happen.

Tawfiq felt the stirring of a deep compassion in his heart for this crumpled-up old woman who did not know when to turn away from the things of the world toward another beauty, another love that is imperishable and ever renewing.

"I have to go now," he said, looking at her in a way nobody else had ever looked at her. There was such kindness in that look that Aliya felt affirmed and loved for who she was beneath her appearance. Though her heart was full of suffering and sorrow, she knew that in time she would be able to endure the truth about the state of her body and its unending desire, surrender to the will of God who has made everything perishable, and turn toward a love that grows with time, a love that would make her younger by the day even as her body disintegrated further into dust.

Then Prince Tawfiq turned from her and went back to his father, a sword in one hand and a shroud in the other. He fell at his father's feet.

"Kill me, Father, for I have erred," he wept. "I deserve no less."

The king lifted him up and embraced him. "I too have erred, Son," he said, wiping away his own and his son's tears.

"I was bewitched by the Witch of Kabul," the prince said.

"The world is the Witch of Kabul, my son. It is our difficult task to always tread the path of truth. Come, your bride awaits you."

And as the prince rode his horse toward his true wife's abode, all the bare trees blossomed and the birds began to sing.

———— ✿ ————

King Kafur does everything we have been talking about in these commentaries to become a conscious and a spiritually evolved human being. He self-examines, questions his feelings and thoughts, digs deep into his soul to discover the causes of his suffering; he pays attention to his dreams, is guided by them, sees and laughs at his own and humankind's folly in swinging between extremes of joy and despair without giving one little thought to the transitory nature of both these experiences. He is so wise he could almost have said Krishna's words to Arjuna in the *Bhagavad Gita*: "The fleeting appearance and disappearance of happiness and distress arise from sense perceptions and we need to learn to bear them both with serenity."

How true. How illusory they both are, and how very *real*, like all appearances. We forget completely the other state when we are in one of them. If we could be serene and watch, instead of getting tangled in and stuck to the ever-changing moods of our mind as we negotiate our lives from day to day, hour to fleeting hour, we would be the most enlightened of beings who take neither state seriously enough to be blown away by it.

But only sages who have replaced pride with humility can unite the contrary states with their unified vision. Only they can build, with the strong, muscular ropes of unfailing memory, a bridge over the chasm between the two hemispheres of their brains. Only they, balanced by remembrance, can walk easily across it at will.

How rare such beings are! Even the wise King Kafur swings like a pendulum. Who are we, foolish, bumbling, and blind, to even envision such steady balance? We do, and indeed must, fail in our endeavors, fall from our perspective perches where we sit as audience to the troubled drama of our lives. Even our failures serve a purpose. If we could be steady without being wise, we would become so proud as to fail again and fall deeper. The interminable climb back up belongs only to the humble and persevering who have faith that with practice and commitment the depth of the fall will become less and less, and their suffering decrease over time.

King Kafur falls far. His fatal flaw is his unexamined and unmeasured attachment to his son. Attachment is at the root of all our suffering and it, along with see-sawing between joy and despair, can spring a garden or blight it.

What is attachment, in a few words? Something and someone we grasp desperately for our own survival; something or someone we think belongs to us instead of to the Power that made it. We can also be attached to ideas, opinions, prejudices, judgments, and beliefs that imprison us in small boxes when our true nature, which is free, wants nothing more than to fly in the vast skies of Mystery and Unknowing.

Attachment must be watched on The Way, so says Rumi and all the guides. Guru Nanak never stops talking about it. He knows that all our suffering comes from this dark, subterranean root burrowing into our minds and hearts. Taoism, Buddhism, Hinduism, Jainism, the Baha'i faith all stress detachment as release from suffering. "The root of suffering is attachment," says Buddha. "Detachment is not that you should own nothing. But that nothing should own you," says the Muslim caliph Ali ibn Abi Talib. An Australian Aboriginal proverb states, "We are all visitors to this time, this place. We are just passing through. We are here to observe, to learn, to grow, to love, and then we return home."

Even though there is a chasm between knowing and implementing detachment, keeping it in mind and reflecting upon it contributes considerably to our peace of mind, happiness, and freedom.

King Kafur forgets it, like most of us tend to do. Wisdom is a shifty thing. Even when we are entirely devoted to living the examined life, to having the enlightened perspective, we fall away from it. Balance is not fixed, but dynamic, maintained by constant shifts, little and sometimes huge adjustments from one state to the other, from folly to wisdom and wisdom back to folly.

King Kafur is so attached to his son that he loses his cool when Tawfiq falls prey to the hag. He does not think to surrender his son to the Being whose child he is but wants to control Tawfiq's fate. He allows himself to be plunged into grief over his son's entrapment. Kafur is blind to the irony that he himself has fallen with his son's fall. If Tawfiq is ensnared by the witch, Kafur is captivated by despair. The king cannot accept that his son has his own destiny that he cannot control.

Who can blame Kafur for his attachment to his son? We are all so attached, and often to people less worthy than Tawfiq, who is a superior man. When we encounter him in the story, he has already traveled far on The Way. Vigilant against the thousand distractions that lie in wait for the wayfarer, he resists with conscious intention Aliya's attempts to ensnare him. But what recourse do we have against circumstance? Whoever we might blame for it, the devil or the universe, this much is certain: All our experiences, whether we judge them as "good" or "bad," are sent to us by Being. Who else is there when Being is All? Even our "bad" experiences have a purpose, as this story shows us. All our characters will travel further on The Way because of them. Even Aliya, it is our hope, will learn that "when the candle of the body begins to perish, one needs to light the candle of the spirit." She too, will embark upon The Way. It is never too late to begin.

But who is Aliya? As a symbol, she is the Illusion of the World, which makes unreal and ugly things desirable. As a character, she is just another of Rumi's unreflecting females. Before I carry on, I have to reiterate here that unconscious women who don't analyze themselves, and are invested in and obsessed with their appearance and sexual appeal, are a creation of patriarchy that disempowers them and denies them the leisure and education to discover them-selves. Have I said this before? It bears repeating.

Aliya is an aging woman teeming with erotic desire. And who can blame her? Don't we all know that though our bodies become decrepit, the heart never ages? Where she goes wrong is in not preparing for and accepting old age. Aren't we given an entire lifetime to do so? Shouldn't she know better than to resist the Way of the World, that which we cannot change with any amount of effort? We deplore her foolishness and feel sorry for her, as we do for our own inability to accept the inevitable. Old age, decay, death are our destiny, which we cannot fight and defeat, and to which we can only surrender in all humility. But which of us can truly say we can do this? Our own failure in this, as in all else, is reason for living in a nonjudgmental, compassionate way.

If the great King Kafur can fall from wisdom, how can we fault poor Aliya? And what hope is there for us?

I too have been struggling with the daily diminishment of my vitality, health, and stamina. My hair, teeth, and height are falling, I have to wear artificial eyes and ears, take pills for those bodily functions that came so naturally earlier, and put more moisturizers on my drying skin. I have many inexplicably bad, dysfunctional days. Have I ceased to struggle with any of this and surrendered my fate? Not entirely.

King Kafur, too, struggled. He took more than a year to surrender his son to his Creator. But we must all eventually do so, or we die like Hamza did, raging till the end.

There is an existential, if not spiritual, necessity for surrendering to that which we cannot change. Most of the world's religions, which are the repositories of humankind's highest wisdom, survival tools gathered over centuries, advocate surrendering to the Cosmic Will. *Islam*, as mentioned before, means "submission"; Christianity's central prayer has the words "Thy will be done"; Sikhism's pivotal message is acceptance of *hukam*, the cosmic command. Deeply connected with the concept of surrendering to God's will is the spiritual law that such a surrendering bears fruit that is far beyond our imagining.

When the singer and harpist Tasleem loses his voice, fame, and harp as he ages, he rages against fate. But it is only when he says to God, "You have given me everything without my asking and taken away from me all that you have given. Take it. It was always yours," that magical things begin to happen to him. As soon as King Kafur remembers through his suffering to surrender his son to his own destiny, help arrives.

Our resistance to surrendering is understandable. The image comes from the literal and metaphoric circumstance of battle and war. When we think about "surrender," we have images of defeat, failure, death. The definitions of the word in *The American Heritage Dictionary* include "to relinquish possession or control of to another because of demand or compulsion"; and "to give oneself up, as to an enemy." It is therefore no surprise that we think surrender undercuts the power of our own God-given free will and makes us puppets of a superior, despotic power.

In the paradox that is life, we humans are both free and bound. There are many things in our lives that we have been given the intellectual, intuitive, and emotional wherewithal to transform and transcend. It is this ability and the will to change our thinking, and hence our lives, that is the strength and power of being human. It is undeniable and sovereign. It is a gift given to us from the cosmos that has created and formed us. It is incumbent upon us to change those things that we want to change and have the ability to change. The Christian serenity prayer says it best: "God, grant me the serenity to accept the things I cannot change, courage to change the things I can, and wisdom to know the difference."

The idea of surrendering becomes relevant only when we come up against limits, both our own and the ones imposed on us by circumstance. Cosmic Will is that which *Is*, that which is unchangeable by any amount of will, strength, effort, or power on our part: Old age, death, loss, the way we look, the culture and race we are born into, our physiology, genes, the immutable arc of our lives, and our fate fall under the "cannot change" category.

Surrendering is not easy. It is the hardest thing to do. It isn't even easy to recognize in one's impatience, anger, frustration, sorrow, and despair that surrendering is the thing to do at a particular moment. But if we don't train ourselves to recognize, see, watch our processes, and listen to the voice of our inner guide, we will perpetuate our suffering by raging where we should acquiesce and accepting what we should fight. Surrender of one sort or another *must* be. If I don't actively assent to my aging, I am surrendering to despair and constant complaining—to being an unhappy and stupid hag, like Aliya, who inhabits my psyche. Surrendering means accepting everything that *Is, as it is.*

The definition of *surrender* most relevant to our spiritual journey is "to give up or give back that which has been granted." We must think of our health and our very lives in this way: a sacrifice to that which has given us everything we have and are.

This giving up and giving back, what we can also call "sacrifice," has to be a regular practice. Without surrendering daily to the small trials of life, we can't hope to surrender easily to the large ones that inevitably call more for greater surrender. I recently lost my expensive hearing aids at the airport in New York. Rather than grow angry that they weren't returned to the Lost and Found, I thought: "Perhaps a cleaner or janitor found them and kept them because she needed them for her mother." Who knows? I'll never know whether they were just tossed into the garbage or put to some use. My not knowing gives me the freedom to think in a way that promotes peace, and makes my loss a giving, a gift.

It is Tawfiq's destiny to fall into the shimmering clutches of the world, into Aliya's clutches. He is on a journey to be able to give himself completely to his wife, to become equal to her in excellence so they can travel The Way together, like the two wings of one bird flying to paradise.

When I reread "The Witch of Kabul," written eight years ago, I felt like a fool for making Tawfiq's bride so perfect. What, not get angry and utterly pissed off when your groom doesn't show up for the wedding? Is she even *real*? Is she even *human*? Guru Nanak and all the gurus and poets in the *Granth Sahib* admit their humanity with unforgiving honesty in their many songs. Humanity, with all its failings, is after all the condition, the very soil, from which our divinity springs. How could I have made Tawfiq's wife such a monstrosity of unblemished perfection?

Now I think there is a purpose for this. She is an idea, an ideal rather than a person, a feminine abstraction that is the bride of Tawfiq's soul. The ultimate marriage, *hieros gamos*, the holy union, we are told repeatedly by our guides, especially the preeminent psychologist Carl Jung, takes places in the temple of our souls. It is the marriage between our lower and higher selves, between human and God. The goal of this marriage is not perfection but wholeness: The human and divine, together, form a whole. We need not, therefore, chide ourselves for or be ashamed of our human failings. They keep us humble, a precondition for proceeding on The Way. As long as we commit to living the examined life, even our folly and forgetting facilitate our movement toward the goal: a little waywardly, a little circuitously, but unfailingly toward our wholeness in which our humanity is balanced by our perfection, and our striving toward perfection tempered by our falls.

Tawfiq will learn from his experience with the Witch of Kabul. Having seen through the illusion of appearance, he will be a good husband to his wife, both person and symbol. His love for her will not be blind, as it was for Aliya. He will have seen through the flames and illusions of worldly passion, which grows hungrier the more it is fed. He will have learned how easy it is for the mind to slip into delusions. He will watch his own and nature's processes even as he participates in them.

CHAPTER 10

THE WORTH OF A PEARL

It seemed to all the courtiers that their king, Mahmud of Ghazni, had become completely mad. In the morning assembly, he took from his pocket a large, lustrous pearl that filled his hand and glowed even in the day. The king put it in his adviser's palm and asked, "What is the worth of this pearl, do you think?"

"I would guess at least a hundred horse-loads of gold," the adviser replied, rubbing his beard.

"Take it."

There was a stunned silence in court. The adviser's fingers closed around the pearl in a tight grasp, but his thrill was nipped in the bud by the king's next command.

"Place the pearl in this mortar and break it with this pestle!"

"B-b-b . . . brea . . . break it?" the adviser stuttered confusedly before he regained his wits and said what he thought he should say. "Your Majesty! How can I . . . how can you . . . the pearl is . . . yours, your highness. I wouldn't dream of taking it. Surely you are testing me to see whether I am a well-wisher of your treasury! I am, my lord, and will not harm this pearl in any way. It will make your highness far wealthier than you already are, and I wish my king the absolute best in financial matters."

The king was somber for a while, and then burst into laughter that was not very genuine.

"Well said, well said, old adviser!" the king said, holding out his hand for the pearl. The adviser reluctantly returned it. "Here is a robe of honor for your loyalty to my treasury!"

The robe was no consolation for the adviser, but he tried not to show his disappointment.

After conducting some business for the day, the king once again brought out the pearl from his pocket, put it in the palm of his treasurer, and asked, "What do you think is the worth of this pearl?"

"At least half a kingdom! May God preserve it from destruction and thieves!"

"Take it."

Having learned from the adviser's example not to take the offer too seriously, but hoping this time the king would let him have it forever, the treasurer closed his claw-like fingers around it.

"Break it!" cried the king again, handing him the mortar and pestle.

"Your Majesty," the treasurer replied, holding the pearl up to the light. "Never in all my life have I seen anything like it, and I have, as you know, seen many gems. Observe this play of light on its surface, its translucent luster, and its color . . . ah, the best, this shade of delicate rose, which is an indication of its incomparable worth. Observe its roughness to the touch. There can be no doubt this is the real thing. And its shape, ah! A perfect sphere. It comes from at least twenty fathoms deep in the sea and weighs, I would say, about fifteen hundred grains. Ah, Your Majesty, nothing like this exists in the whole world! Break it? Why, I would sooner break my head!"

The courtiers laughed, and after another gloomy silence, King Mahmud joined in the laughter.

"I am surrounded by people who value my treasury! What a boon!" the king said. "I am surrounded by intelligent, practical men bent upon my good. Ah, my treasurer, what poetic, descriptive talents you have! How shall I reward you for saving me this wonderful pearl? Here's a carriage with six white horses for your very own."

The king wearily conducted more business, signed more papers and discussed plans for another conquest. But once more he returned to the subject of the pearl. This time he put it in his commander's palm and told him to take it. The commander, too, clutched the pearl in the hope the king would let him keep it. Hadn't he served and loved the king well? He certainly deserved it. But having learned from the example of the others what his response to the king's insane command should be, he prepared his answer. When the king commanded him to break it, he waxed poetic over the pearl's worth and beauty, and he too was rewarded handsomely for it.

So the king approached all his officials, and all of them preserved the pearl, and all of them received rich rewards and raises in salary. Feeling dejected, the king was about to retire for the day when he noticed a ragged-looking young man in a torn and patched sheepskin jacket and worn-out shoes standing in the entryway of his court. His lustrous, curly dark hair hung in ringlets about his face, which had a translucent glow like the nacreous shine of the new moon.

"And what's your name?" the king asked.

"Ayaz, sire," the man bowed low in respect.

"And what do you want, Ayaz?" the king asked.

Ayaz dropped to his knees before the king, held his hand, kissed it, and said, "To love, serve, and obey you, sire!"

"How much do *you* think this pearl is worth?" the king said, dropping the pearl into Ayaz's tough and leathery hand.

"More than I can imagine or say," Ayaz replied.

"Here, put it in this mortar and break it into fragments with this pestle."

Without a moment's thought or doubt, free of anxiety and fear of consequences, oblivious to reward or punishment, Ayaz brought the pestle down with a powerful movement of his hand, and smashed the pearl to a dusty powder.

The people in the court gasped in shock and prepared to arrest Ayaz.

"You have broken the king's invaluable pearl!" they cried. "Infidel! Uncouth, ignorant fool! Enemy of the king! Kill him! Kill him!"

The king's many ministers pounced on Ayaz and would have finished him off if the king hadn't intervened.

"Release him!" cried King Mahmud.

The officers reluctantly let him go. The poor shepherd looked even more ragged and disheveled in his now-torn sheepskin jacket.

"What do you have to say for yourself, young man?" the king asked.

"Princes, renowned officials," Ayaz said. "Is the king's command more precious than a pearl? Your gaze is fixed upon the pearl, not upon the king. Compared to his command, this pearl is just a stone."

The king's eyes lit up with joy, and all exhaustion fell away from him. He walked over to Ayaz and, his dirty outfit notwithstanding, held him near his heart, and whispered: "Here is my heart, my Ayaz, my pearl, my treasure. I have found you!"

———— ❀ ————

When we use words like *worth* and *value*, we generally mean material goods: gems, houses, cars, clothes, money. Any circumstance that threatens to diminish our "wealth" causes us untold misery and anxiety. We spend all our lives preserving, guarding, increasing, and grasping our possessions. Like the courtiers, we think this is all that matters. And indeed, such an mind-set gets us rewards: more goods, acclaim, robes of honor, a carriage with six horses, Porsches and BMWs, and the envy of everyone else. These make us comfortable, rich, satisfied; they elevate us in our own eyes and in the eyes of the world. We think these things *should* matter to us simply because they matter to others. Like the courtiers, we imitate others and others imitate us, till our entire social fabric is based on a constricting web of mimicry. This noose of our own making becomes tighter and we lose perspective, that most precious of our gifts.

There is nothing wrong with loving material possessions. We are hardwired to do so. They arouse our admiration because they are pleasing to our senses. Besides, they can give us a lot of joy, comfort, and opportunity for engagement. It is only when we forget that we must never allow them to possess us, that the true values of courage and detachment serve us better than our possessions do, that they become obstacles on The Way.

The courtiers mistakenly believe that the king has the same values as they do. That we see our own traits in another, in a process called "projection," is another truth we neglect at our own peril. In other words, people are mirrors that show us our own reflections. The guides told us of this long before the phenomenon became a psychological term. "Many an iniquity you see in others is your own nature reflected in them, O reader," Rumi says.

The courtiers think the king's concern is primarily the priceless pearl, which they themselves lust after, and that the king is testing their loyalty to his pocketbook.

On one level the king is testing his officials' detachment from material possessions, from objects that they collectively esteem as precious. But as a representative of the King, Creator, and Destroyer of Everything There Is, he values nothing. Brilliant men and women die, treasures are sunk to the bottom of the sea. Earth, water, wind, and fire wreak havoc on habitations and lives. He holds nothing sacred, views nothing as irreplaceable. What is the worth of a pearl to the Owner of Everything?

The courtiers can't see through the king's "madness"; they do not have the psychological insight to see what He is truly seeking: someone who will respect Him enough to obey him; someone who will love him enough to surrender everything to His Will.

Surrendering does not imply a passive giving up of something. Our dharma, karma, and circumstance often call upon us to break things: give up possessions, like so many wealthy Jains do at some point in their lives in a ceremony called *diksha*, which comes from the Sanskrit word meaning "to give up" or "destroy," like the Buddha who renounced a kingdom. We often have to give up more than material possessions; we have to terminate relationships when they grow toxic, give up and cut off our own limbs if necessary for our greater good and health, and surrender peace for the imperative of battle.

Sometimes we are called upon to destroy or sacrifice something that we think is ours, or something we think defines us—an idea, a concept, a value, a principle. Often, without our knowing it, they are just unexamined prejudices. We also have to surrender our versions of "God" and battle our own definitions and preconceptions. No matter how broad a vision we have of the Mystery, it is inevitably constricted by our own limitations. Our battles with God are often projections of our battles with our own small selves. In our story of Moses, the shepherd's small version of God as an embodied being had to disintegrate before he could find the Mystery.

Undoubtedly, surrendering to the Cosmic Will calls upon us to destroy. Destruction and creation, chaos and order, are inextricably one, though we separate them in our efforts to understand them. There wouldn't be one without the other. "In things spiritual there is no division and no numbers," Rumi says. In our striving for nonviolence and peace, which in themselves are much to be desired, we often forget this fundamental fact of existence. New growth springs from the mulch of a tree felled by a thunderstorm; trees exist because other trees have died to make room for them; we exist because our ancestors have died to make space for us. We have hands and feet and organs because of the programmed death of cells in the process called "apoptosis," without which we would not have forms and shapes: We have fingers and toes because the cells between the digits have destroyed themselves. Without this death we would have webs and blobs instead of hands and feet.

Think about Krishna's words to Arjuna on the battlefield in the *Mahabharata*. Arjuna's courage falters as he realizes that the people he is fighting with and about to kill are his cousins, uncles, and nephews, and Krishna gives him the great lesson of the *Bhagavad Gita*, which has resounded down the ages. Among the many pearls of wisdom from the *Gita* that give us deep insight into our true nature is this one, relevant to our discussion: "Performing the action prescribed by our nature is no sin."

Our primary duty is to be fearless inner and outer warriors, to fight with all we have, even if it means destroying whatever stands in the way—brothers, families, friends, and sometimes even one's own life. Fighting takes its toll, but the price of not fighting is far higher.

But I have strayed far from our story and must return to it.

Enter Ayaz, and the story turns from its literality to Truth. Though he is ragged and poor, has none of the signs of "success" and "wealth," Ayaz is the wealthiest of them all in the true sense of "value" and "worth." He is the only one in this story who knows how to destroy what everyone else considers invaluable. He is the warrior and devotee par excellence—detached from all but the One. All he desires is to love and serve his King of Everything. He knows beyond doubt that what the king truly desires is not things, but that obedience which is an integral part of love; that love in whose service we must be prepared to surrender everything.

Ayaz doesn't take an instant to reflect, self-examine, and doubt. Ayaz does not know why the king, symbol of that Power, often seemingly autocratic, imperious, senseless, asks him to smash the pearl; he does not consider the consequences of this action for himself. He only knows that he must obey.

And the only worth and consequence of obedience that truly counts is love, devotion, worship. As God tells Moses in the story of the shepherd, "What do I gain from worship? Nothing! Prayer and worship are kindnesses I have bestowed on my creatures so they may be tied to me with chords of love." That there are material consequences of this love in terms of health, wealth, and happiness is both wonderful and beside the point. We know from other stories Rumi wrote about Ayaz that he becomes incredibly wealthy. We also know that his wealth, instead of corrupting him, makes him all the more humble. He makes himself a sacrifice to the will of his king.

Sacrifice and surrender are intimately connected. Recall the definition of surrender as "giving up or giving back that which has been granted." Everything we surrender to the One when we are called upon to relinquish it, or when it is forcibly taken away from us, comes back to us a thousandfold, materially and spiritually. The King of Kings has gifted us in uncountable ways, as the following two stories show. It is incumbent upon us, in Guru Nanak's phrase, to "eat the given" as we move through the seasons of our lives of which apoptosis—the shedding, or "falling off," as of leaves—is a part.

CHAPTER 11

AND THIS BELONGS TO...

A clever old wolf was always hungry. There simply wasn't enough prey in the jungle in which he lived, and though the mountains above were teeming with food, the many lions there were a threat to his life. So he came up with a clever strategy to satisfy his hunger. He planned to make an alliance with the head lion, king of the wilderness. He would also enlist the aid of his neighbor, the poor fox. United, they would go on a hunt to the dangerous mountains where there was plenty of prey. Their combined efforts would ensure success.

The wolf went to his neighbor, the thin and straggly fox who had a mate and many offspring. The little ones, exhausted from hunger, gave up on trying to play and lay around looking sad and thin. The wolf explained his plan to the fox, and added, "You'll have plenty of fresh, warm meat for yourself and your family! Come, join me in this venture!" The hungry fox was easily convinced, and became his ally.

Together the wolf and the fox approached the majestic and grand lion, who lay outside his lair, taking a snooze in the sun.

"O king of the jungle and of the mountains, we have come to you with a plan," the wolf said.

The lion heard them out, got up, roared, and stretched. He offered his services to satisfy the hunger of his supplicants.

Up in the mountains they had no trouble finding prey. The fox found the animals with his sense of smell, the wolf circled and trapped them, and the lion killed them easily. Together they brought down a mountain ox, a fat boar, and a wild goat.

As they dragged the dead animals down the mountainside, the hungry wolf and the fox wondered if the lion would share the spoils of the hunt with them. They feared the lion would eat the kill all by himself and not leave anything for them. Hadn't they participated in the hunt? Would the lion have succeeded without their help? Their fears alternated with hope that the lion would be just, and divide the meat fairly amongst them.

They piled their booty in the center of a clearing in the forest, and the lion said to the wolf, "O wolf, be my assistant and divide this prey amongst the three of us. And be just."

"What could be easier?" thought the wolf. Aloud, he said, "O big and strong king, the large and hefty mountain ox is yours, the boar is mine, and the goat belongs to the fox."

Having said this, the wolf, who had no doubt in his mind that he had done the fair and just thing, stood proudly aside. The fox too was very pleased with this judgment, though he didn't show it.

"Is that your final decision?" the lion asked.

"Yes, Your Majesty," the wolf replied, bowing before him.

"When I am here," the lion roared, his voice resounding through the forest, "how can you speak of 'I' and 'you'?"

Then the lion pounced on the wolf and tore him to bits with his fierce claws.

The fox shivered inside his fur as he watched in horror his neighbor being shredded to pieces before his eyes.

"You, fox, go ahead now, and divide this prey for our breakfast."

The fox had a moment of terror, and then a flash of insight flared in his brain. He bowed low before the lion, and said, "This fat ox will be your breakfast, O wonderful king! And this juicy boar will be . . . your lunch. And this plump goat shall be . . . yours, O bountiful king, for supper."

"And what about you?" the lion asked.

"Everything is yours, O king! You alone have made this abundance possible. Without you, none of this would have come to be. It is only in your mercy that all the creatures of this forest live and flourish. I am but a small part of you, and entirely yours. What you give me I shall eat, and what you withhold, too, shall be a gift."

"Who taught you your wisdom, O fox?"

"You did, O glorious king, and . . . the fate of my unfortunate neighbor, the wolf."

"Ah, then take all three animals, for they are yours. Since you have become entirely mine, I am you and you are me. How then can I deprive you of anything?"

The lion turned around and walked to his lair. The fox thought to himself, "A hundred thousand thanks to the lion for asking the wolf first to make the division. If he had asked me first, how would I have escaped with my life, and all this bounty? How fortunate we are to come into this world after those who have gone before us, so we can take warning from their fate."

———— ✦ ————

Need and hunger, for all sorts of things, make us turn to the lion for aid.

Some rationalists say God is just a feudal concept, a carryover from our collective history when we bowed and scraped to authorities who held the power of life and death over us; that fear is at the root of all our worship— "I'll be humble and meek, so please don't tear me to pieces as I have seen you do to others. Please protect me, take care of me and mine."

There is certainly some truth in this way of thinking. When we hear the wolf's judgment, in which he gives the biggest portion of meat to the lion, we think, "Why, that's very fair, indeed." We are as shocked as the fox when the lion turns around and shreds the wolf to tatters. We also shiver in our shoes, fearing a similar fate. Haven't we heard and read about, been witnesses to, in our own lives and on TV—which brings the lives of others to our doorstep— the terrible and frightening fate of others? As of the poor wolf's?

Many of us depend upon "God" in times of need. Many do not admit this dependence and are even ashamed of their secret reliance upon this Power. But according to a Gallup poll, nine out of ten Americans believe in God or a universal spirit. We are wiser than our rationality. Our collective roots burrow far beneath our conscious minds to suck sustenance from the center of the fruiting earth and the cosmos that speak to us of Presence everywhere we look. We need only to open our eyes, minds, and souls, to expand our reflection and our vision to see it and feel it. We need look no further than our own lives, bodies, and minds to be aware of it.

"Something saves me every day from falling down the stairs, tripping at the curb, being blindsided," says James Hillman, the renowned psychologist and thinker, in his book *The Soul's Code*. "How is it possible to race down the highway, tape deck singing, thoughts far away, and stay alive? What is this 'immune system' that watches over my days, my food sprinkled with viruses, toxins, bacteria?"

Our lives, our breath, the functioning of our bodies and minds—so mind-bogglingly complex that scientists of all eras have been baffled by them—are gifts bestowed upon us by the universe. We forget all this when we fear and suffer. Then all we can do is suffer and disbelieve. It is important when we speak of God and our many gifts to remember the dark side of our existence, which we cannot dismiss, deny, or understand. Weariness, despair, depression, conflict, hunger, desire, dread—there is no way around our humanity! They are all part of our reality. Admitting our own suffering and helplessness gives us humility and the softness of soil that is ready for all sorts of seeds, all sorts of possibilities.

But I was speaking about fear. I have never written or spoken about it, and fear being a large part of "And This Belongs to . . . ," I will avail myself of the opportunity to reflect upon it.

When I observe my own fears, I find that most of them have to do with imagined scenarios of the future rather than what is happening *now*. Most of my fears surface in the middle of the night, when I am most vulnerable. I fear the failing of my mind, by which I lay so much store. I fear dying without accomplishing my many tasks; I fear ill health and physical pain. As Mark Twain is often credited with saying, "I've had a lot of worries in my life, most of which never happened."

Those who say, like William Faulkner in his acceptance address for the Nobel Prize in Literature, "The basest of all things is to be afraid," have a point. There are many things we should not be afraid of, even though it is understandable that we are. We are afraid to speak out against powerful interests. Religions that do not tolerate dissent and whose adherents kill those who disagree with their positions—an increasing phenomenon in our times—elicit our fear as well, the biggest of which is fear of death.

Specifically, the Mystery we do not and cannot know, the great Circumstance that sends us bolts from the blue—and who among us has not experienced the turning of our lives in a second, whether through a sudden death or accident—holds our lives and the lives of those of we love in Its hands. Our ancestors used to perform sacrificial acts to propitiate It. Human sacrifice was a part of all cultures from the very beginning of human society, and animal sacrifice is well and alive in many parts of the world today.

I do not endorse this sort of sacrifice. It is altogether too primitive. It is also the easy way out. Kill something else to propitiate your own fear. We have evolved a great deal from those times when we projected and dealt with our fears outwardly.

We have not evolved out of fear because it too has a function in our lives. As *The Dhammapada: The Path of Perfection* says, "Those who fear what they should not fear, and who do not fear what they should fear . . . go the downward path." Fear is a survival tool. It keeps us alert and alive physically and mentally, for there are many dangers that lurk in our behavior and the slippery slopes and sinkholes of our minds.

The fox knows from the wolf's death that it is wise to fear the Mystery we worship. It is this fear that keeps us in our place. Icarus did not fear, flew too high toward the sun with his waxen wings, and plunged to his death. Too much complaining about our lives and conditions is not healthy and healing, although a whine every now and then feels good! We forget when we complain too frequently that there is so much more we can lose, that things can be so much worse than they are. Guru Arjan, the fifth guru of the Sikhs, says in his marvelous song *Sukhmani Sahib* (*Prayer of Peace*), "For everything you complain about, He can take away ten more from you. What, fool, will you do then?"

The King demands nothing less than the sacrifice and surrender of our whole being; surrender to the point where there is no difference between the King and us. When we consider that even our breath is not ours, we must acknowledge that *everything* we are and have is a gift—not outright, but a loan. At some point we must "give up or give back that which has been granted." But that point begins, or ought to begin, far earlier than when it is wrenched away from us perforce. As Kabir says, *nothing* is ours. "When I return to you what is yours, what remains of me?" We have to teach ourselves to hold in loving guardianship everything that we possess, from material goods, talents, health, and people to our lives themselves. It is in this context that the wolf in his "just" division goes wrong in his thinking, and the failure of this recognition destroys him.

The wolf is clever. To satisfy his hunger he makes a pact with the lion. You give me this and I will give you that. It is a business arrangement for him. He believes his own efforts will bring him success in his endeavor. It is this sort of reliance on our own cleverness that both Rumi and Guru Nanak warn us against.

The fox, on the other hand, though also hungry, seems content with his hungers till the wolf reveals his plan. After the hunt both the wolf and the fox fall prey to doubt. They fear the lion will renege on his word and leave them nothing. Their labors would have been wasted. They want the lion to be fair and just.

Fairness and justness, as we saw in Hamza's demands in *The Dark Flower of Justice*, is a value we humans live by. Even when we deny it to others, we expect it for ourselves. The lion too wants the wolf, to whom he gives the task of dividing the prey, to be just. The wolf finds this to be an easy task. He will give the largest share to the lion. Who can quarrel with that? But both the animals have forgotten that the Giver is the Giver and Maker of everything there is. In giving them sustenance, He is giving them life. Their lives, their existence, their hungers are all owed to Him. His expectation is that we realize that "I" would not be here if it weren't for "You." He wants the kind of love and devotion in which we sacrifice our own small "selves" to become a part of the Self that is All.

Guru Ravidas, a low-caste saint whose compositions are included in the Sikh holy book, the *Granth Sahib*, says in one of his songs: "You are me and I am You. What is the difference? As gold and a gold bracelet, as the ocean and a wave." In another song, Kabir says: "When 'I' am, You are not. Now You are, and I am not. You and I are One." "There is no room in the house of God for two 'I's," Rumi says.

The Creator and the creature are not separate. This is where The Way leads us: this merging, this Oneness, this lack of separation between origin and born.

It is this understanding the fox attains because of the rude shock and fear he feels at the fate of the wolf that, in a way, was a sacrifice for the fox's enlightenment. Yes, it is clever on the fox's part to learn from his neighbor's lack of vision, but it is not just cleverness and cunning. In that moment he *gets* it— not just that the lion makes it all possible, but that he is a small part of the lion himself, that he belongs to Him. That he will eat whatever is given him to eat.

We are enriched, not impoverished, by this surrendering. One of my all-time favorite poems is the long narrative poem "The Hound of Heaven," by Francis Thompson (1859–1907). The poet flees from the Hound of Heaven, God, who pursues him, he thinks, to deprive him of all the things of the world that he desires: women, love, children, nature, and wealth. He suffers a great deal in his flight "down the labyrinthine ways of my own mind," and his experiences yield him a harvest "dunged with rotten death." But God catches up with the poet, who is wearied from his flight from Him, and the Voice, which has been speaking to him all along, says: "Lo, all things fly thee, for thou fliest Me!" The Voice chastises the poet for fleeing Him, and utters some of the most moving lines in the poem:

> *Whom wilt thou find to love ignoble thee*
> *Save Me, save only Me?*
> *All which I took from thee I did but take,*
> *Not for thy harms,*
> *But just that thou might'st seek it in My arms.*
> *All which thy child's mistake*
> *Fancies as lost, I have stored for thee at home:*
> *Rise, clasp My hand, and come!*

The poet understands that his gloom has been the shadow of His hand "outstretched caressingly." He hears the words:

> *Ah, fondest, blindest, weakest,*
> *I am He Whom thou seekest!*
> *Thou dravest love from thee, who dravest Me.*

———— ✿ ————

I am reminded of this poem by the last part of the story, in which the lion gives the fox all the spoils of the hunt and says to him: "Since you have become me, how can I deprive you of anything?"

Such wealth surrender bestows.

CHAPTER 12

THE SWEETNESS
OF BITTER MELONS

Though Luqman was a slave, he was a master of himself because he was free of anger, lust, resentment, greed, and pride. His enlightened king, Hamid, who could discern the difference between chaff and grain and appearance and truth, had seen through Luqman's outer role to his inner state, and loved him dearly. King Hamid was quite weary of the constricting role of master, and found great joy in humble service to his slave and beloved, Luqman.

King Hamid would have set Luqman free a long time ago, but Luqman did not want to be free. Whenever the king went to a place where he was not known, he would place Luqman on his personal horse and travel behind him on an ass, like a slave. King Hamid would put his own clothes on Luqman, wear the latter's clothes, and serve him. When the king's cooks prepared feasts for him, or when his friends and subjects brought him delicacies from all over the world, he would feed Luqman with his own hands before partaking of the food himself. His greatest delight was eating Luqman's leftovers. If Luqman did not eat, the master would also forgo his food. Such was his love for his slave.

One day, King Hamid received a basket of the best melons from Punjab, in India. They were reputed to the sweetest in the world, and when cut, their insides were the brightest saffron. Before tasting any himself, King Hamid sent for Luqman, and when he arrived, seated him on a cushion on the king's own chair. When the master cut a slice and gave it to Luqman on a golden plate, Luqman ate it with such relish, such slurping of its juices, that everyone present craved a slice too. The master gave him another slice, and Luqman ate it the same way. The master continued to offer him slices, and Luqman continued to eat them with great pleasure.

When Luqman was satisfied, King Hamid decided to eat some himself.

As soon as the king bit into the melon, however, his face puckered up with distaste and he spat it out. His tongue was blistered and his throat burned with the fruit's bitterness. He threw his hands up in pain and distraction, and cried out to his slave:

"Oh, how did you eat this again and again? Why didn't you complain? How did you turn so much poison to sweetness?"

"From your generous hand and bounty, O master," Luqman replied, "I have received so many gifts. Tell me, how can I complain about one bitter thing?"

"But how could you endure the bitterness of slice after slice?" the master asked.

"With love, my master, bitter things become sweet. With love iron becomes gold, pain becomes healing, the dead man made living," Luqman replied.

"And a burdened king becomes a joyous slave," said King Hamid, bowing before Luqman, and kissing his feet.

———— ✿ ————

The reality of slavery, which still exists in pockets of the world and lurks subliminally in our minds, is a blight on humanity, undeniably abhorrent. We need to delve deep into ourselves and explore the dark roots of our desire for control over fellow humans, paid employees, servants, women, partners, husbands and wives, and extirpate it without mercy. It is a law of the universe that we will not receive compassion, kindness, and love unless we first teach ourselves to give it.

The literal fact of slavery, where one human being regards another as a beast of burden, an inferior being to be manipulated for gain and comfort, however, is just one of the many-layered concepts of slavery that has seeped into the entire spectrum of our consciousness from the beginnings of our history. The poles of Enslavement and Ruling are in our psyches as metaphors that manifest in many subtle and not so subtle ways.

"Who ain't a slave?" asks Ishmael in Herman Melville's *Moby-Dick.*

It is a question worth asking ourselves in order to see the many ways in which we are in bondage: to our appetites, compulsions, complexes, habits of body and thought, our very "natures" that we do not even think about changing to our benefit; to our many needs and fears, to others, to appearances, unexamined principles, prejudices, and values; to people, money, success, and material goods; to our relationships with parents, children, family, and friends. Most of our bonds, though they give us a lot of joy, also entangle us and are the source of conflicts and suffering.

Being bound is the human condition. We cannot avoid

servitude, slavery. But the word *bond* has multiple meanings: It can mean a fetter, a shackle, or a uniting force or tie; a link. Both meanings are present in our relationships. Our misery often comes from conflicted relationships, but we cannot live without interpersonal bonds.

The questions we really need to ask are: If I must be so attached, what is the one thing most worthy of being attached to? Which bond at once connects and liberates? Under whose subjugation am I a king?

Guru Nanak says plainly that without the uniting force of Love, which is yet another name for the Mystery, all our other relationships and connections are garbage. Without love for this Love in our hearts, our relationships will not be fruitful. Quite the contrary. It is almost as if this Love is a precondition for all love. Love begets love. Attachment to people without this Love creates conflict, power struggles, impossible expectations. In fact, attachment and love are mutually exclusive. Attachments turn our gifts and endowments into curses. But when we are connected to the One Love, all our other bonds become conscious, voluntary, free—sources of joy, comfort, and connection. This Love detaches us, in time, from all our other attachments by giving us a perspective on them. "Choose the Love of that Living One who is everlasting, who gives thee to drink of the wine that increases life," says Rumi.

King Hamid and Luqman's relationship shows us the way to Love.

Luqman has polished his heart through deep introspection, self-examination, self-control. He has become the master and ruler of the vast territories of his psyche, subduing the many demons lurking in the shadows of his unconscious mind: lust, anger, envy, pride, and all the monsters they spawn; he has harnessed with attention and intention his attachments to the many things that would hijack his quietude and his ability to love and serve.

Though a master, Luqman knows that where the king, figure-head of the King of Kings, is concerned, he is a slave and wants to be nothing else. Luqman knows that it is only in his slavery to the king who rules from the kingdom within him that he is free. His awareness of the manifold gifts, literal and perceptual, that he gets from this slavery, keeps him in this humble space. For it is only with utter humility that he can approach, access, and be in the Presence of this king.

Luqman's slavery to the king is what frees and detaches him from the contrary qualities of sweetness and bitterness. Luqman knows that the other name of this type of slavery is Love. "In this world the bitter sea and the sweet sea are divided," Rumi says. "Know that both these flow from one origin. Pass on from them both, go all the way to their origin!" This detachment from our "good" and "bad" experiences is the truest of freedoms. When we examine ourselves closely, as under a microscope, we can see quite clearly the magnified truth that it is our attachment to what we consider "good," "pleasant," and "pleasurable," and our fear of the "bad," that is at the root of all our suffering. When we consider that it is the "bad," the suffering, which goads and whips us into finding ways of transcending it, leads us to self-examination, and gifts us the sight and insight that we develop on The Way, we can see how in the paradox that is life "good" can be bad, and "bad" good. As Guru Nanak says, there is healing in suffering and disease in peace. In Rumi's words, suffering is both "poison and antidote."

Luqman does not refuse the bitterness of the melon from Punjab, nor complain about it. By accepting it, he makes it sweet. He accepts it because it comes from the Hand of the Beloved. And every bitter experience, no matter whose hand offers it, comes ultimately from the Hand of the Beloved.

Guru Arjan, the fifth guru of the Sikhs, did not simply say "Thy will be done," but rather, "Thy will be *sweet.*"

Legend has it that Mira Bai, the iconoclastic sixteenth-century saint, was sent a chalice of poison by her royal in-laws for associating with male saints. She drank it and began to laugh. Similarly, Luqman's love for and attachment to the Mystery transcends life and death; his is an ever-willing sacrifice to the Love that has transformed him from a slave to a king. There is nothing he will not eat or drink from the hand of his king.

Let's admit that surrendering is not easy. Even Christ cried out to the Father as he hung on the cross; even Guru Arjan, who was tortured and executed by the Mughal emperor Jahangir for not converting to Islam, says, "It is easy to speak and talk, but it is difficult to accept Your Will." What hope is there for us mortals? Crying out in bitter suffering, too, is our condition and destiny. But without practicing this surrender in small and big ways, we will keep suffering meaninglessly and drown in bitterness. The struggle to surrender, to become slaves of the Mystery, to attach ourselves to it must be kept alive because the stakes are high, and the goal is Love.

Luqman is the Arch Lover. Luqman, we know from other stories Rumi has told about him, is externally an ugly man whom Love has made beautiful beyond compare.

King Hamid's capacity for love is abounding. He is no mortal king but a metaphor for the Magnanimous Majesty with so many different names that we worship and call upon in our hours of need. This symbolic story gives us a glimpse into the character of this king, Ruler of the Universe, ever ready to become his own subject. His gaze tears through appearance to the heart of Luqman, the perfected slave, sees himself reflected in its polished mirror, treats him as a king, and loves him.

There is such sweetness in this subjugation—imprisonment, if you will—that even King Hamid wants to be the slave of his slave. He too wants to experience the highest emotion given to us to experience—the ecstasy of love. We need only look within ourselves, at our culture, movies, books to see how important it is for us humans. It is the warp of all our desiring. It is our frustration and our undying hope till the very end.

It is to experience this ecstasy that the king so happily and secretly plays at being a slave and lover. He wears Luqman's clothes, rides his donkey, eats his leftovers; he goes wherever Luqman, soul of his soul, goes. In short, he *becomes* Luqman, just as the ocean becomes the river that empties into it, and vice versa. Master and slave become one for the sake of Love. As Rumi says in another story, in another context, "The souls of both were knit together without sewing."

It is to experience this, the ecstasy and pain of Love, the Sikh gurus say, that the Mystery inhabits, participates in, and becomes each corner and cell of the human body, head, and heart. It is for this ecstasy that the Mystery weaves itself into the very fabric of our lives, suffering with our suffering, rejoicing in our joy, loving through our loves.

There is never any separation in surrender. There is never any separation, ever. Separation exists only for those of us who do not hunger to connect—the hunger that Nanak says is fulfillment in itself. "Through Love," Rumi says, "the earthly body soars to the skies; the mountain becomes nimble and begins to dance."

Love, of which our loves are reflections, moons to the sun, is another name for the immaterial, unseen, ungraspable quintessence of existence that we call God.

The Way is the Way of Love, then; the Love that reveals itself and enters the hungry, adoring heart; the Love that transforms our suffering into joy, our poison into a life-giving elixir; the Love whose bonds and cords set us free.

"Hail O Love," says Rumi,
"that brings us good gain—thou art the Physician of all our ills."

AFTERWORD

I am a lover of Rumi, rather than a scholar of his work. These reimagined stories are a labor of love. And indeed, the labor has been considerable, joyous, and immensely rewarding. The source of these stories—Rumi's six-volume *Mathnawi*, written in Persian and translated into English by Reynold A. Nicholson beginning in 1925—is a dense, intimidating text, somewhat like a huge mountain rich with deep caves of precious stones and hidden veins of shimmering gold. My exploration and excavations have been tremendously enriching and instructive, and I hope the reader will find these stories equally rewarding.

While growing up in India, I had heard Rumi's name, together with those of other Muslim saints and poets like Kabir, Sheikh Farid, Sheikh Bhikhan, Hafiz, Mirza Ghalib, and Iqbal, among others. While residing in the United States, too, I had heard and seen Rumi's name more and more frequently over the years.

When I moved into my husband Payson Stevens's house shortly before our wedding, I saw in his library a copy of the three varicolored volumes of the *Mathnawi*. It was part of a larger collection of books from almost all the spiritual traditions of the world, bequeathed to Payson by his friend John Phetteplace, a photographer, composer, and cellist who died in 1992. I eyeballed the *Mathnawi* and flirted with the idea of reading it one day. But, too much else was happening and I simply could not afford the luxury of reading a voluminous body of work.

Once I took the books off the shelf, dusted them, and read the first line of the very first volume—"Listen to the reed how it tells a tale, complaining of separations"—I was hooked. This was Krishna's flute calling to my busy, hitherto deaf soul, awakening it, and reminding it of the journey it came here to make. And this call was coming to me, not from my own Sikh tradition, not from Hindu mythology that I explored in my book *Ganesha Goes to Lunch*, but the Islamic Sufi tradition. I am an eclectic at heart, and glean ways to follow The Way, no matter the tradition or culture.

The first line of the *Mathnawi* aroused a hunger in me for more. I read a page. So much jostled and stirred in such a small space: longing, agony, feelings balanced by thought, thought tempered by emotion, images that opened doorways in the mind and heart. There were no boundaries or distinctions between Rumi's head, heart, and soul—they merged, aiding one another on his journey, which was as certain as a river in its direction. There was a world here, in each word, in each image. There was a love that was physical and transcendent, material and mystical. I knew right away that this was not going to be a flirtation, but a lifelong marriage.

In 2003, I retold one of Rumi's stories, "The Prison and the Rose Garden," for the journal *Parabola*. Retelling one story wasn't enough; but it had to do. I knew that more was in store, although I didn't quite know what.

In 2006, after I had finished writing *Ganesha Goes to Lunch,* I knew I wanted to write similar books for all religious traditions. My first book on Rumi, *Rumi's Tales from the Silk Road,* was followed by *The Singing Guru: Legends and Adventures of Guru Nanak,* from the Sikh tradition.

When my father, who always strove to remember and practice the fundamental Sikh reverence for all paths, died in April 2007, I turned to Rumi for solace. Death is always a call to adventure, and Rumi's three volumes were calling to me. When I returned to India, where Payson and I now live for half the year, I knew I had to begin working on Rumi's tales. I felt a leap of joy in the midst of my grief.

Rumi is well known as a poet. Few know he is a master storyteller. Perhaps the reason why Rumi is less known for his considerable narrative skills is his manner of telling tales. His meandering style—which lends support to the theory that the *Mathnawi* was dictated—was better suited to an age that had time, or rather, a different concept of time. To Rumi, time only appears to be linear and continuous, but is, in fact, circular and ever-renewing. Rumi's manner of telling his tales, like his concept of time, is also circuitous, meandering, concentric, eccentric. His stories are habitually interrupted by other stories, long discourses and digressions, rhapsodies, poetic flights, expositions, and the colloquies and dialectics of a multidimensional soul with itself.

Rumi is very aware of his style, and often even critical of it. A thousand times he scolds or laughs at himself for it: "This discourse hath no end. Go; relate the conclusion of the tale." Or, "This digression has passed beyond bounds." But Rumi's apparent shortcomings are precisely his greatness. We can see in the *Mathnawi* the organic process of a great mind in action. It is clear that if consciousness has a form, it is akin to the form of trees and rivers—nonlinear, with many branches, tributaries, and distributaries. His stories, too, reflect this structure.

In his self-awareness as a writer grappling with the material of the human psyche, shapeless thought, and feeling, Rumi is very modern. Every writer must encounter the limits of his material, and Rumi confronts his head-on. Being a metaphysician, he knows such limits are intimately tied to the limits of language and all its devices—figures of speech, images, symbols, parables—and beyond, to the very nature of all matter and life. Words, images, and metaphors take us this far on The Way, and no further. The transcendent Rumi knows there is a point beyond which his stories cannot go. "The old man has shaken his skirt free from talk and speech. Half of the tale has remained in his mouth," Rumi says at one point. But the artistic Rumi, the storyteller and poet, pushes back the boundaries of the inexpressible again and again, and utilizes his material to perfection. He makes it very clear that all his stories, in fact, all images and words are faces, masks of the godhead. Rumi uses this analogy long before Joseph Campbell formulated his thesis about masks that both manifest and conceal the godhead. The function of masks is to take the writer—and the reader—through the sensory sphere of ordinary human experience to that Unseen dimension beyond human thought and conception of which our sensual world and everything in it, including us, is a sign and symbol.

Ultimately, in Rumi's works, there remains no division between the secular and the sacred, the literary and the spiritual. In his expert hands, literature is a tool for the expression of the spiritual. The manner and matter of writing become the path on which he takes himself and the reader to that Ocean of Being into which all empties and from which all returns.

Rumi's stories are a marvelous mix of excellent storytelling and spirituality. In his stories, Rumi's social self predominates: the Rumi who is engaged with the drama of relationships—between lovers, husbands and wives, fathers and sons, guides and disciples, humans and God and destiny—and above all, the relationship of the human soul with itself, or rather, its Self. Embedded in the secular lives of humans, these dramatic narratives hold up a mirror and give form to our inner selves, reflecting that amorphous existence we lead beneath the level of conscious thought that determines all our reality, the quality of our life, and the extent of our suffering.

Rumi's themes invariably revolve around those human thoughts, desires, cravings, and actions that go against the Cosmic Will. The working of this Will unfolds in the ineluctable and unchangeable Way of the World, what the old world called destiny, or God's will, or that which Is.

The notion of destiny is central to the greatest literature of the West—all Greek and Shakespearean tragedies are threaded with it. We are inclined to dismiss it as no longer relevant to our technologically driven lives. In our resolve to march forward into a science that we believe will find solutions to all our ills and fix the unfixable, we have buried and left "destiny" behind. We think of it as a prison and cannot see how an acknowledgment of its limits can liberate us to experience love and joy.

All Rumi's stories demonstrate the limits of the human will divorced from and at odds with the Will of the Universe, that which has to happen. Most of the characters in these stories persist in ways that create and perpetuate their suffering. They imprison themselves further and further in their attempts to extricate themselves from That Which Is. Those who learn the imperative lesson of prayer, humility, and surrender will enter the Rose

Garden of Paradise. Those who don't will perish or undergo intense suffering, which is another gateway to the Garden.

Sufis venerate suffering, and Rumi emphasizes that all suffering is a gift. Its redemptive purpose is to turn us toward the Light and Love of that suprasensuous and Unseen (though everywhere evident) energy, ubiquitous in and around us.

The Unseen and suprasensuous substratum of all reality, common to the philosophies, theologies, and experiences of both East and West, can only be accessed, Rumi says, in times of loss and tragedy, by the eye of the heart: "The water of life is hidden in the land of darkness."

AKNOWLEDGMENTS

Thanks are due first and foremost to Tessa Murphy, my excellent editor at Mandala Publishing, who has encouraged, supported, championed, and improved this book with her insightful editing. And to Raoul Goff, yet again, for my fourth title with Mandala. What a blessing to have their support!

ABOUT THE AUTHOR

Kamla K. Kapur is the author of *Ganesha Goes to Lunch*, *Rumi's Tales from the Silk Road*, and *The Singing Guru*. Kapur has also published two books of poetry, *As a Fountain in a Garden* and *Radha Sings: Erotic Love Poems*, numerous short stories, and a series of award-winning plays. She divides her time between the Kullu Valley in the Indian Himalayas and Southern California.

MANDALA
PUBLISHING

An Imprint of MandalaEarth
PO Box 3088
San Rafael, CA 94912
www.MandalaEarth.com

Find us on Facebook: www.facebook.com/MandalaEarth
Follow us on Twitter: @MandalaEarth

Library of Congress Cataloging-in-Publication Data available.

ISBN: 978-1-68383-490-8

Publisher: Raoul Goff
Associate Publisher: Phillip Jones
Creative Director: Chrissy Kwasnik
Designer: Ashley Quackenbush
Project Editor: Tessa Murphy
Associate Managing Editor: Lauren LePera
Senior Production Editor: Rachel Anderson
Production Manager: Sadie Crofts

ROOTS of PEACE   REPLANTED PAPER

Mandala Publishing, in association with Roots of Peace, will plant
two trees for each tree used in the manufacturing of this book. Roots
of Peace is an internationally renowned humanitarian organization
dedicated to eradicating land mines worldwide and converting war-
torn lands into productive farms and wildlife habitats. Roots of Peace
will plant two million fruit and nut trees in Afghanistan and provide
farmers there with the skills and support necessary for sustainable
land use.

Manufactured in China

10 9 8 7 6 5 4 3 2 1